Heal.. Dont Cry

44 Ways to Heal

Heal.. Dont Cry

44 Ways to Heal

By

Madhura Girish

Published by - Self- Published
Publishers Add - India
Printers details - India
Edition Details - First

TABLE OF CONTENT

Introduction — *i*

Why This Book Can Change Your Life — *iii*

Healing—What It Really Means & Why It Matters — *ix*

Who Needs Healing? Signs You Might Be Carrying Hidden Wounds — *xiii*

What Happens If We Don't Heal? The Silent Cost of Unresolved Pain — *xvii*

Energy Healing Explained—The Science & Magic Behind It — *xxi*

How to Use This Book: A Guide to Your Self-Healing Journey — *xxv*

Part 1 Understanding Your Pain & Breaking Free — 1

The First Step: Facing Your Pain Without Fear — 3

Emotions Are Energy—How Your Feelings Shape Your Reality — 5

The Hidden Wounds of the Past—How Trauma Still Affects You — 8

Breaking Negative Thought Patterns—How to Stop the Spiral of Overthinking — 11

Why Crying is a Superpower—The Science of Healing Through Tears — 14

Part 2	**44 Ways to Heal**	**17**

Mind & Emotional Healing: Heal from the Inside Out — 19

Healing a Broken Heart—Step-by-Step Guide to Moving On — 21

Affirmations That Rewire Your Mind for Strength & Peace — 25

How to Rebuild Confidence After Rejection or Failure — 29

The Art of Forgiveness—A Simple Practice That Sets You Free — 33

How Visualization Can Heal Your Pain & Manifest a Better Life — 35

The Dustbin Method—A Trick to Instantly Let Go of Negative Thoughts — 37

Breaking Free from Perfectionism—Stop the Self-Sabotage — 39

Inner Child Healing—Heal the Younger You That Still Hurts — 42

Energy & Spiritual Healing: Clear Blocks & Raise Your Vibration — 47

Crystals for Healing—How to Use Amethyst, Rose Quartz & More — 49

The Healing Power of Reiki—Recharge Your Mind, Body & Soul — 51

Energy Cleansing Rituals—Smudging, Salt Baths & Sacred Incense — 55

Cleansing Your Aura—Simple Daily Rituals for Protection & Peace — 58

Cord Cutting—How to Break Free from Toxic Relationships — 61

Karmic Blocks—Are Your Past Energies Holding You Back? 64

The 44 Karmic Lessons—What Your Soul is Trying to Learn 67

Daily Energy Detox—A Powerful Routine for Emotional Balance 71

Lifestyle & Environmental Healing: Detox Your Space, Detox Your Soul 75

Protect Your Energy—How to Cut Off Negative People 77

Declutter Your Home & Mind—Why Cleaning Up Changes Everything 80

Sacred Spaces—How to Create a Healing Corner at Home 83

Morning Healing Rituals—Start Your Day with Strength & Peace 86

The Healing Power of Silence—How Quiet Time Clears the Mind 89

Becoming the Best Version of Yourself—A Roadmap to Inner Peace 91

Stop Touching the Wound—How to Let Go of Pain for Good 95

Alternative Healing & Transformational Techniques: Unlock Hidden Healing Powers 99

Full Moon Rituals—How to Release What No Longer Serves You 101

Healing Through Travel—Why a Change of Place Can Change Your Life 104

Oracle & Angel Cards—How to Use Them for Clarity & Guidance 108

EFT Tapping—A Simple Technique to Heal Emotional Pain   111

The Magic of Gratitude—How to Shift Your Energy Instantly   115

Seeing the Bigger Picture—How Self-Reflection Can Heal You   118

Unfollow, Unfriend, Unsubscribe—Why Digital Detox is Self-Care   121

Spiritual Practices for Inner Peace— Meditation, Prayer & Stillness   124

Color Therapy—How Colors Affect Your Mood & Energy   127

Who You Spend Time With Matters—How to Choose the Right People   131

Talking to a Healer—When & Why You Might Need Professional Help   135

Trusting the Universe—How to Let Go & Believe in Divine Timing   138

Manifesting Miracles—How to Rewrite Your Story with Faith   142

Building a Healing Routine—A Simple Daily Plan for Lifelong Peace   145

How Spirituality Heals—The Connection Between Faith & Well-being   148

Becoming a Healer: Transform Your Pain into Purpose   153

Becoming a Healer—How to Turn Your Healing Into a Career   155

Sharing the Gift—Helping Others & Creating a Ripple Effect   157

The Mission: A Healer in Every Home— 159
Changing the World, One Soul at a Time

Final Chapter   163

The Path Ahead - Your Healing Never Ends, 163
It Evolves

How Healing Transforms Your Life—A 165
Personal Reflection

The Continuous Journey of Growth—What 167
Comes Next?

Resources & Tools for Lifelong Healing— 170
Where to Go from Here

Introduction

A Journey to Your Best Self

There comes a moment in life when you realize something needs to change. Maybe it is a quiet whisper inside you, a feeling of restlessness, or a deep knowing that you are meant for more. Or maybe it is a loud, undeniable pain—heartbreak, loss, disappointment—that forces you to stop and ask, Is this really how my life is meant to be?

If you are holding this book, it is no coincidence. Something inside you is ready to heal. Something inside you is ready to awaken.

Healing is not just about fixing what is broken; it is about uncovering who you truly are beneath the layers of fear, pain, and self-doubt. It is about returning to the wholeness that has always been within you. And most importantly, it is about stepping into a life where you no longer just survive— but truly live.

Why This Book is Different

This is not just another self-help book. This is not a book that will tell you to "just be positive" or "move on" from your pain. This is a book of deep transformation. It is a companion on your healing journey, a guide that will walk with you through every stage of your growth.

Each chapter in this book offers a powerful yet simple way to heal, whether it is emotional wounds, mental blocks, or energy imbalances. But more than just reading, this book invites you to experience healing firsthand. Some chapters will challenge you, some will comfort you, and some will shift your perspective in ways you never expected.

You do not need to read this book in order. You can open any page and find wisdom, tools, and exercises that speak to exactly what you need at this moment. Because healing is not linear—it is a journey that unfolds in its own time, in its own way.

Who This Book is For

This book is for you if:

- You have been carrying emotional pain and are ready to release it.

- You feel stuck in patterns of self-doubt, overthinking, or fear.

- You have experienced loss, heartbreak, or trauma and want to heal.

- You are curious about spirituality, energy healing, or self-discovery.

- You know you are meant for something greater but feel unsure of how to step into it.

This book is for the seekers, the healers, the dreamers, and the souls who are ready to awaken to their full power.

What You Will Discover

In this book, you will explore:

- **Understanding Your Pain** – Why past wounds still affect you and how to release them.

- **Healing Techniques That Work** – 50 transformative ways to heal your mind, body, and energy.

- **Practical Exercises & Rituals** – Simple yet powerful daily practices to integrate healing into your life.

- **The Deeper Truth About Healing** – How to move

beyond just "feeling better" and step into true emotional freedom.

- **Becoming the Best Version of Yourself** – How healing is not just about the past but about creating the future you desire.

This is not a book to be read and forgotten. This is a book to be lived.

A Personal Invitation

I invite you to read this book not just with your mind, but with your heart. Let it be a space where you reflect, release, and rediscover yourself. Healing is not about perfection; it is about progress. It is about allowing yourself to feel, to grow, and to trust that everything you need is already within you.

As you turn these pages, know that you are not alone. Every person who has ever healed has stood where you stand now. And every person who has ever transformed has done so by taking one brave step at a time.

Let this book be your first step. Or your next step. Or the step that finally changes everything. Are you ready? Your healing journey starts now.

Why This Book Can Change Your Life

Have you ever wished for a way to heal—truly heal—from the pain that lingers in your heart and mind? The kind of healing that doesn't just help you "cope" but actually frees you? If you've picked up this book, it means a part of you is searching for relief, for clarity, for something deeper than just temporary solutions.

This book is different...

It's not just about "feeling better" or masking your emotions. It's about **transforming your pain into power.** It's about **clearing the wounds you've carried for too long—**whether from heartbreak, childhood trauma, stress, loss, or simply the exhaustion of life's challenges.

Healing Isn't About Forgetting—It's About Becoming Whole Again

Healing doesn't mean erasing the past. It means learning how to make peace with it so that it no longer controls your present. It means giving yourself the gift of **freedom from emotional baggage.** Most of us carry silent wounds—painful experiences, regrets, broken relationships, fears, and self-doubt. And because we never learned how to process them properly, they continue to affect our choices, our relationships, and even our health.

But **what if healing could be simple?** What if, instead of feeling overwhelmed, you had a guide—one that gave you clear, practical, and deeply powerful ways to heal?

This book is that guide.

Why This Book Will Transform You

Unlike traditional self-help books that make healing feel complicated, this book is designed to be:

- **Easy to Follow** – You don't need to read it in order. Pick any chapter, any healing method, and start your journey from there.

- **Deep Yet Simple** – Every concept is explained in a way that's easy to understand but profound enough to make a real impact.

- **Practical & Actionable** – Each chapter gives you real healing techniques that you can start using immediately—whether it's emotional release, energy cleansing, or shifting your mindset.

- **For Everyone** – Whether you're new to healing or already on your spiritual path, these methods are for you.

Healing Isn't a One-Time Event—It's a Journey

There's no "one-size-fits-all" method to healing, which is why this book offers 50 different ways to help you find what works best for you. Some methods will be deeply spiritual, others purely psychological, and some will be rooted in daily habits. You'll discover ways to:

- **Let go of emotional pain** and stop reliving past wounds.

- **Rebuild your confidence** after setbacks, rejection, or loss.

- **Cleanse negative energy** from yourself and your surroundings.

- **Cut ties with toxic relationships** that drain your peace.

- **Use simple techniques** like affirmations, visualization, crystals, and color therapy to shift your energy instantly.

- **Learn how to listen to your own inner wisdom** and trust life's process.

Healing is not about perfection. It's about progress.

If you allow yourself to fully experience the wisdom in this book, you will begin to feel a shift—not just in your mind, but in your energy, your relationships, and your entire life.

Your Healing Begins Now

You don't need to wait for the "right time" to heal. You don't need anyone's permission. Healing is your birthright. And it starts **now.**

Are you ready?

Turn the page. Your journey to wholeness is waiting...

Healing—What It Really Means & Why It Matters

When you hear the word healing, what comes to mind?

For many, healing sounds like something only physical—like recovering from a wound, a fever, or an illness. But **true healing goes far beyond the body.** It's about the mind, emotions, and even the energy we carry within us. Healing is **not just about fixing something that is broken**—it's about restoring balance, peace, and strength within yourself. It's about feeling whole again.

Healing Is Returning to Your Natural State of Peace

You were not born with fear, self-doubt, guilt, or emotional scars. These things were picked up along the way—through experiences, relationships, and struggles. Healing is the **process of unlearning pain.** It's about peeling away layers of hurt and confusion to return to the **peaceful, powerful being** you were always meant to be.

It's **not about erasing the past**—but learning how to carry it without suffering.

It's **not about becoming someone else**—but uncovering the strength and wisdom already inside you.

It's **not about pretending everything is fine**—but about facing the truth with courage and compassion.

The Invisible Wounds We Carry

Not all wounds are visible. Some of the deepest pain exists within us—hidden behind smiles, work, distractions, and daily routines.

Maybe you've experienced:

- **Heartbreak** that still lingers in your chest.

- **Rejection** that made you feel like you weren't enough.

- **Loss** that left an emptiness you don't know how to fill.

- **Fear of failure** that keeps you from pursuing what you truly want.

- **Childhood wounds** that still shape how you see yourself.

These wounds may not bleed, but they weigh us down. They affect our relationships, our confidence, our decisions, and even our health. **Healing is the key to setting yourself free.**

Why Healing Matters—The Price of Ignoring Your Pain

Many people believe that **time heals all wounds.** But **time alone does not heal—only intention and action can.**

Ignoring your pain doesn't make it disappear. It buries it. And buried pain has a way of resurfacing in the form of:

- Anxiety, stress, and overthinking.

- Feeling stuck in life, like something is holding you back.

- Repeating unhealthy relationship patterns.

- Lack of confidence and self-worth.

- Physical symptoms like exhaustion, headaches, or body aches.

When we don't heal, we stay trapped in cycles of pain.

But when we choose to heal, we **break free.** We open ourselves to love, clarity, and a sense of lightness we may not have felt in years.

Healing Is for Everyone—Not Just Those Who Are "Broken"

Healing is not just for people who have been through extreme trauma. **It is for everyone.**

Even the happiest, most successful people have inner wounds. The difference is—some choose to face them, while others ignore them. Healing is an **act of self-love.** It is choosing to no longer let the past define you. It is deciding to move forward lighter, stronger, and with more clarity.

And the best part? **You don't have to do it alone.**

This book is your guide—a collection of powerful, practical ways to help you heal in a way that feels right for you. Whether it's through energy healing, self-reflection, emotional release, or spiritual practices, **you will find something here that speaks to your soul.**

You Deserve to Heal. You Deserve to Feel Free.

You do not have to carry your pain forever.

Healing is possible. It is real. And it is waiting for you.

Are you ready to take the first step?

Turn the page, and let's begin.

Who Needs Healing? Signs You Might Be Carrying Hidden Wounds

Healing is not just for those who are visibly struggling. It's not just for people going through heartbreak, trauma, or grief. Healing is for everyone...

We all carry something—some form of pain, fear, self-doubt, or emotional baggage. And because we've learned to "live with it," we often don't even realize how much it's affecting us.

But here's the truth:

- If something inside you still feels unsettled... you need healing.

- If a past event still weighs on your heart... you need healing.

- If you feel stuck, lost, or emotionally exhausted... you need healing.

The Hidden Signs That You Might Need Healing

Not all wounds are obvious. Some are buried so deep that we mistake them for "just the way life is." But the signs are there—if we choose to see them.

Take a moment to see if any of these resonate with you:

- **You feel emotionally exhausted, even when life is "fine."**

Sometimes, everything looks good on the outside, but inside, you feel drained, uninspired, or numb. This could be a sign that unresolved emotions are weighing you down.

- **You keep attracting the same kind of toxic relationships.**

If you find yourself in repeating cycles of heartbreak, betrayal, or toxic connections, it might be because there's an unhealed wound that keeps drawing you toward the same patterns.

- **You struggle with self-doubt and never feel "good enough."**

If no amount of achievement or praise makes you feel truly worthy, it could be a sign that an old wound is still influencing how you see yourself.

- **You avoid thinking about the past because it's too painful.**

If certain memories make you shut down or feel overwhelmed, it means there's something within them that still needs healing.

- **You feel like you're stuck in life, unable to move forward.**

Whether it's in relationships, career, or personal growth, feeling stuck often means there's emotional baggage holding you back.

- **You have physical symptoms that don't have a clear medical cause.**

Unhealed emotions can manifest as headaches, fatigue, body aches, or even digestive issues. Your body is always speaking to you—listen to it.

- **You struggle to let go of anger, resentment, or guilt.**

If certain situations or people still trigger a strong emotional response in you, it's a sign that the wound hasn't fully healed.

The Truth About Pain: You Don't Have to Carry It Forever

Pain is not meant to be a life sentence. It is meant to be processed, learned from, and then released. But many of us do the opposite—we bury it. We distract ourselves. We keep moving forward, hoping time will erase the wounds. It doesn't.

Time only buries pain deeper—until one day, it shows up as anxiety, overthinking, emotional numbness, or self-sabotage.

How Healing Can Transform Your Life

Imagine waking up without heaviness in your chest.

Imagine relationships that feel healthy and fulfilling.

Imagine making choices from a place of confidence, not fear.

Imagine feeling free, light, and truly at peace.

That is what healing gives you.

It doesn't mean life will be perfect. It means you will no longer carry the same old wounds into your future. It means you will finally feel whole again.

Healing is a Gift You Give Yourself

If any part of this chapter resonated with you, take it as a sign: Your soul is ready to heal.

And the best part?

Healing doesn't have to be complicated.

In the next chapters, you'll discover 50 powerful, simple ways to start your healing journey—one step at a time.

Are you ready? Let's begin.

What Happens If We Don't Heal? The Silent Cost of Unresolved Pain

Most people believe that if they ignore their pain long enough, it will eventually disappear.

But pain doesn't just fade—it waits.

It settles deep inside, showing up in ways we don't even recognize: in our habits, our relationships, our fears, and even our bodies. Unhealed wounds don't stay in the past. They keep whispering in the present, influencing our decisions, our emotions, and our overall well-being.

If we don't heal, we don't just "stay the same." We slowly become someone weighed down by the past, even if we don't realize it.

The 7 Ways Unhealed Pain Controls Your Life

1. You Keep Repeating the Same Painful Patterns

Have you ever noticed that certain struggles seem to follow you?

- The same toxic relationships.
- The same feelings of unworthiness.
- The same self-sabotaging behaviors.

This isn't a coincidence. When we don't heal, we unconsciously recreate familiar pain, even when we don't want to. It's as if the wound inside us attracts similar experiences over and over—until we finally choose to heal it.

2. Your Mind Becomes Your Own Worst Enemy

Unhealed pain doesn't just stay in your heart—it takes over your thoughts.

- Overthinking.
- Self-doubt.
- Anxiety that keeps you up at night.
- That nagging voice telling you, "You're not good enough."

Healing isn't just about feeling better—it's about reclaiming peace of mind so that your thoughts no longer work against you.

3. Your Body Stores the Pain

Pain that isn't healed doesn't disappear—it moves into the body.

- Unexplained fatigue.
- Chronic tension in the shoulders or neck.
- Headaches, digestion issues, or even heart palpitations.

The mind and body are deeply connected. When emotions are buried instead of healed, they manifest physically. This is why so many people feel exhausted even when they haven't done anything physically tiring.

4. You Struggle to Trust & Open Up to Others

Unresolved wounds make us guarded. They teach us that vulnerability is dangerous, that people will hurt us, and that it's safer to keep our emotions locked away.

But the truth is: Healing doesn't just restore you—it restores your ability to love and be loved.

5. You Feel Stuck, Like Something Is Holding You Back

You want to move forward. You want to grow. You want to experience life differently.

But something keeps pulling you back.

That "something" is often an unhealed wound—one that quietly tells you that you don't deserve better, that you're not ready, or that change is too scary. Healing allows you to break free from those invisible chains and finally step into the life you deserve.

6. You Numb Yourself Instead of Facing the Pain

When we don't heal, we often look for ways to escape the pain instead of processing it.

This can show up as:

- Scrolling mindlessly through social media.
- Overeating or undereating.
- Distracting ourselves with work.
- Addictions to alcohol, shopping, or even toxic relationships.

These things don't actually heal us. They just temporarily silence the pain—until it comes back louder.

7. Life Feels Heavy, Even When It Shouldn't

Have you ever had a good day, but still felt a lingering sadness? Or achieved something great, yet still felt empty inside?

That's the weight of unhealed pain.

It keeps joy at a distance. It makes happiness feel temporary. It convinces you that no matter how much you have, something is still missing.

But the truth is: You don't need more achievements or distractions—you need healing.

Healing Is the Only Way to Break Free

The good news? You don't have to live like this forever.

Healing is not about "fixing" yourself—you are not

broken. It's about releasing what no longer serves you.

You deserve to:

- Wake up without emotional heaviness.
- Feel light, free, and at peace.
- Have relationships that feel safe and fulfilling.
- Trust yourself and your decisions.
- Live without carrying the weight of old wounds.

The Time to Heal Is Now

You've carried this pain long enough.

Now, it's time to put it down.

In the next chapters, you'll discover powerful, simple ways to start healing—practices that will help you release emotional weight, clear your energy, and step into a lighter, freer version of yourself.

Are you ready? Turn the page, and let's begin.

Energy Healing Explained—The Science & Magic Behind It

Have you ever walked into a room and instantly felt uncomfortable, without knowing why? Or met someone whose presence made you feel calm and safe, even before they spoke?

This is energy. And whether we realize it or not, it affects everything—our emotions, our health, and even the way we experience life.

But here's the part most people don't know: Energy can be healed.

What Is Energy Healing?

Energy healing is the process of clearing, restoring, and balancing the energy within and around you so that you feel lighter, stronger, and emotionally free.

Unlike traditional healing, which focuses only on the body or mind, energy healing works on a deeper level—the level of vibration, frequency, and unseen forces that shape our reality.

Just like the body has a physical system (nerves, blood, organs), it also has an energy system. This includes:

- **Your Aura** – The energy field that surrounds you.

- **Your Chakras** – The energy centers in your body that influence emotions and health.

- **Your Vibrational Frequency** – The level of energy you emit, which attracts similar energies into your life.

- When these are clear and balanced, you feel:
- **Mentally peaceful** – No overthinking, no emotional chaos.
- **Emotionally light** – No heavy energy weighing you down.
- **Physically strong** – More energy, fewer unexplained aches and pains.
- **Spiritually connected** – A sense of trust in yourself and the universe.

But when they're blocked or unbalanced, you might experience:

- Feeling tired or drained for no reason.
- Repeating the same emotional struggles.
- Attracting negative people or situations.
- A sense of heaviness, sadness, or unexplained anxiety.

This is why energy healing is so powerful—it removes what no longer serves you so that you can fully step into your power.

The Science Behind Energy Healing

Even though energy healing is often seen as "spiritual," it has a strong scientific basis.

- Your body is made of energy. Every cell, organ, and thought carries an electromagnetic charge. When energy flows smoothly, we feel balanced. When it gets blocked, we feel stuck—mentally, emotionally, and physically.

- Your thoughts and emotions create vibrations. Studies in quantum physics show that thoughts and emotions emit energy frequencies. Positive thoughts create high vibrations, while negative ones create low, dense energy. This is why healing the mind is just as important as healing the body.

- Your body stores emotions as energy. Trauma, stress, and negative experiences leave energetic imprints in the body, affecting your health and emotions until they're released.

This is why energy healing techniques like Reiki, breathwork, meditation, and cleansing rituals work—they help clear out stuck energy so that you can heal faster and deeper.

Signs You Need Energy Healing

Not sure if your energy needs healing? Look out for these signs:

- You constantly feel drained, no matter how much you rest.
- You feel anxious or low, even when nothing is "wrong."
- You attract toxic people or situations repeatedly.
- Your home or workplace feels heavy, making you uneasy.
- You struggle with self-doubt, fear, or inner negativity.
- If any of these sound familiar, it's time to clear your energy.

How Energy Healing Can Transform Your Life

When you heal your energy, everything shifts:

- Your mind becomes clearer.
- Your emotions become lighter.
- Your relationships become healthier.
- You attract more positive experiences.
- You feel truly free, as if a weight has lifted.

You Can Heal Your Own Energy

The best part? You don't need to be a healer to heal yourself.

This book will guide you through 50 powerful ways to heal, including:

- **Crystals** – How to use them for emotional balance.

- **Aura cleansing** – Simple ways to remove negative energy.

- **Chakra balancing** – Activating your inner power centers.

- **Releasing energy cords** – Freeing yourself from toxic connections.

- **Daily energy rituals** – Small habits that create huge shifts.

Healing your energy isn't complicated. It's about small, powerful changes that create lasting transformation.

Your Healing Starts Now

The energy you carry shapes your life.

If you're ready to clear out what no longer serves you and step into a lighter, freer, and more empowered version of yourself, turn the page.

Your healing journey has already begun.

How to Use This Book: A Guide to Your Self-Healing Journey

Most books tell you to read them from the first page to the last. But this book is different.

Healing isn't a linear journey—it's deeply personal. Some days, you'll feel ready to do deep emotional work. Other days, you'll need something simple and soothing. That's why this book is designed for you to use in the way that feels right for you.

You don't have to follow the chapters in order. You can flip to any chapter, find what speaks to you, and begin there.

Some sections will challenge you. Some will bring clarity. Others might stir emotions that you've been avoiding. That's all part of the process. Healing is not about forcing yourself—it's about meeting yourself where you are.

Finding What You Need, When You Need It

Here's how to get the most out of this book:

- If you're feeling stuck and don't know where to begin... Start with the section on acknowledging pain and understanding how emotions shape your reality. These chapters will help you identify what's holding you back and why healing is necessary.

- If you're struggling with emotional pain, heartbreak, or self-doubt... Dive into the Mind & Emotional Healing section. These chapters will help you rebuild your self-worth, break negative thought patterns, and release emotional pain.

- If you're dealing with low energy, negativity, or unexplained exhaustion... Go to the Energy & Spiritual Healing section. Learn how to clear your aura, balance your energy, and remove toxic attachments.

- If you feel lost, overwhelmed, or disconnected from life... The Alternative Healing & Transformational Techniques section will give you new perspectives—helping you connect with your intuition, spiritual strength, and inner wisdom.

- If you want long-term healing and growth... The Lifestyle & Environmental Healing section will help you build a healing-friendly life—one that naturally supports your emotional well-being.

No matter where you start, the key is to start.

A Book That Grows With You..

Healing is not a one-time event. It's a journey that unfolds in layers.

There will be days when you feel strong and empowered. There will be days when emotions hit unexpectedly. That's okay. That's healing.

This book isn't just for reading—it's a companion to guide you through those moments. You might read a chapter today and find new meaning in it months later when you've grown.

That's how healing works. You're constantly evolving.

You Don't Have to Do This Alone

Healing can feel overwhelming, especially if you've spent years suppressing your emotions. But remember this:

- You are not broken. You are simply carrying energy that is ready to be released.

- Healing isn't about fixing yourself. It's about returning to who you were meant to be.
- You are never alone in this journey. Millions of people are healing alongside you.

Let this book be your safe space, your guide, and your reminder that you are capable of transformation.

No matter how lost or broken you feel right now, healing is always possible.

Now, let's begin.

PART 1

UNDERSTANDING YOUR PAIN & BREAKING FREE

The First Step: Facing Your Pain Without Fear

Most people want to heal—but few are willing to face their pain.

It's not because they don't want to get better. It's because pain is uncomfortable. It's easier to distract ourselves with work, social media, or endless to-do lists than to sit quietly and acknowledge what's really happening inside. But here's the truth: **you cannot heal what you refuse to feel.**

Healing doesn't begin when you "get over" something. It begins the moment you stop running, take a deep breath, and turn toward your pain—not as an enemy, but as a messenger.

Pain That Hides Itself

A few years ago, I met a woman named Meera during a healing retreat. She was warm, always smiling, and seemed to have her life together. But when she spoke about her childhood, her voice would tremble just a little, her fingers tightening around the cup of tea she held.

One evening, after a group meditation, she broke down crying. "I thought I was okay," she admitted. "I thought if I just kept moving forward, kept working hard, kept pretending the past didn't matter, I'd be free from it."

But she wasn't. And neither are many of us.

Pain that isn't processed doesn't disappear—it buries itself deeper. It shows up in different ways: in the relationships we attract, in the way we speak to ourselves, in the fears that hold us back.

Meera had done everything "right"—a successful career, a loving family, a stable life—but inside, she still carried the unspoken grief of a childhood where she never felt truly seen. And it was exhausting her.

Maybe you've felt that way too. Maybe a part of you is tired—not from the weight of life itself, but from the energy it takes to suppress what needs to be healed.

Why We Fear Facing Pain

Pain isn't just an emotion. It's a survival response. Our minds are wired to avoid it, to escape anything that feels too overwhelming. It's why people keep themselves busy, why they scroll endlessly on their phones, why they tell themselves, "I'm fine" even when they aren't.

But ignoring pain doesn't heal it. It only traps it inside you. And the longer it stays, the more it shapes your life in ways you don't even realize.

The Moment Everything Changes

Something happens when you finally stop and acknowledge what's been hidden inside. The moment Meera let herself cry that night, something shifted. She wasn't just "having a breakdown." She was having a breakthrough.

She wasn't as afraid anymore.

Because that's the thing about pain—it's scarier in our minds than it is in reality. When we finally face it, we realize that we are stronger than we thought. That we can sit with our emotions without breaking. That we can observe our past without letting it define us.

Healing doesn't mean drowning in emotions. It simply means giving yourself permission to say:

"Yes, this hurt me. Yes, I am still affected by it. But I am ready to release it now."

How to Gently Face Your Pain Without Overwhelm

You don't have to relive old wounds all at once. Healing is not about forcing yourself to feel everything immediately. It's about small, safe steps toward awareness.

Maybe today, it's as simple as taking a deep breath and whispering to yourself, "I am safe."

Maybe it's writing down a memory that still feels heavy and noticing how your body responds.

Maybe it's placing a hand on your heart and simply sitting with whatever emotions come up, without judging them.

The point is not to rush. It's to start.

Because the moment you stop running from your pain, you take away its power over you. And that's when healing begins.

Your First Step Starts Now

Right now, by reading these words, you've already begun your healing journey.

You are no longer avoiding. You are acknowledging. And that is more powerful than you realize.

There is nothing wrong with you. You are not broken. You are simply carrying emotions that are ready to be released.

And the more you allow yourself to feel, the lighter you will become.

Emotions Are Energy—How Your Feelings Shape Your Reality

Have you ever walked into a room and immediately felt the tension, even though no one said a word? Or met someone whose presence instantly made you feel at peace? That's energy at work.

Everything in this world carries energy—including **your emotions.**

But most people don't realize just how much their emotions shape their reality. The way you feel doesn't just affect your mood—it affects your choices, your relationships, and even your physical health. The energy you carry influences everything around you.

If you've been feeling stuck, drained, or emotionally exhausted, it's not just "in your head." It's in your energy field. And until you learn to shift that energy, life will keep reflecting it back to you.

The Hidden Power of Your Emotional Energy

Think of emotions like frequencies on a radio. Love, joy, gratitude, and peace vibrate at a high frequency. Fear, anger, guilt, and sadness vibrate at a lower frequency.

When you're filled with joy and gratitude, you radiate high energy. People are drawn to you, opportunities flow, and life feels easier. But when you're carrying unhealed pain, anger, or fear, that energy weighs you down. It creates resistance, attracts similar low-frequency experiences, and keeps you stuck in cycles of negativity.

This is why two people can face the same situation but have completely different experiences—because their **internal energy determines how they perceive and respond to life.**

A Story of Energy Shifting Everything

I once worked with a man named Rohan, who came to me feeling completely lost. He was frustrated with his career, felt invisible in relationships, and was constantly drained.

At first, he believed external circumstances were to blame—his boss, his colleagues, his family. But when we dug deeper, he realized that for years, he had been carrying **deep resentment** from a past betrayal.

That unhealed energy made him guarded. It made him doubt people's intentions, close himself off, and unknowingly push away the very things he wanted—love, success, and happiness.

The moment he started releasing that energy—through forgiveness, breathwork, and emotional clearing techniques—things changed. People began treating him differently. Work opportunities opened up. He felt lighter, and for the first time in years, **life stopped feeling like a battle.** Nothing outside of him changed. But because he shifted his **internal energy,** his entire reality followed.

Your Energy Creates Your Life

Right now, the energy you carry is shaping the experiences you attract.

If you constantly feel exhausted, ask yourself—what emotions are draining me?

If you keep attracting the same toxic relationships, ask—what unhealed wound is keeping me in this cycle?

If you feel stuck, ask—what emotions am I holding onto that are keeping me from moving forward?

Your emotions are not random. They are messages. And when you learn to listen to them, you gain the power to change everything.

How to Shift Your Emotional Energy

You don't need to force yourself to "be positive" all the time. That's not healing—that's suppression. Real healing happens when you learn how to process emotions instead of being controlled by them. Start small. Right now, take a deep breath and notice how you feel. No judgment, just awareness.

If you're carrying heaviness, ask yourself, What is this emotion trying to tell me?

If a negative thought arises, pause and ask, Is this really true, or is this just a story I've been repeating?

Every small moment of awareness shifts your energy.

And as your energy changes, your life will begin to change too.

You Are More Powerful Than You Think

You are not at the mercy of your emotions. You have the power to shift your energy, to heal what weighs you down, and to create a life that feels light, free, and aligned.

Everything starts within you.

And now that you know this, you will never look at your emotions the same way again.

The Hidden Wounds of the Past—How Trauma Still Affects You

You may not think about it every day, but the past lives inside you. Not just in memories, but in the way you react, the way you trust, and even the way you love. Unhealed wounds don't just sit in the past; they shape who we become. They whisper fears into our decisions, create patterns we don't understand, and sometimes, keep us stuck in cycles we don't know how to break.

Have you ever wondered why certain things trigger you so deeply? Or why do you struggle to feel safe in relationships, even when nothing is wrong? That's the past speaking. And if we don't acknowledge it, it continues to control us.

The Pain We Carry Without Realizing It

I once had a conversation with a woman named Ananya. She was independent, successful, and confident on the outside. But in her personal life, she was always afraid that people would leave her.

If a friend took too long to reply, she assumed she had done something wrong. If someone she loved seemed distant, she felt abandoned, even though nothing had actually happened.

When she looked deeper, she realized this pattern had followed her since childhood. As a little girl, she had often felt invisible—never truly heard, never reassured. And now, as an adult, those wounds still dictated her emotions, making her feel unsafe even in relationships that were completely healthy.

This is what trauma does. It doesn't just exist as a memory—it becomes a **belief** about the world.

How Unhealed Trauma Shapes Your Life

Even if we don't consciously remember painful moments, our body and subconscious mind store them.

- If you were criticized often as a child, you might struggle with self-worth as an adult.

- If you experienced betrayal, you might find it hard to fully trust people, even when they've done nothing wrong.

- If you grew up in instability, you might fear change, always needing control to feel safe.

Trauma is not just the big, obvious events like abuse or loss. It can also be **the small, repeated moments where you felt unseen, unheard, or unworthy.**

And if we don't heal these wounds, they continue to replay in different forms—until we finally face them.

Recognizing Your Emotional Triggers

One of the biggest signs of unhealed trauma is **overreacting to small things.**

Not because you are dramatic, but because **something deep inside you is being touched.**

- A casual comment makes you feel deeply hurt.

- A small rejection feels like a massive loss.

- Someone pulling away makes you feel like you are

about to be abandoned.

These reactions aren't about the present moment. They are old wounds being reopened. **The emotions feel bigger than the situation because they are coming from years of unprocessed pain.**

Breaking Free from the Past

The past does not have to define you. Just because something hurt you once doesn't mean it has to hurt you forever.

Healing starts when you begin to **separate the past from the present.**

Next time you feel triggered, pause. Instead of reacting, ask yourself:

"Is this emotion about right now, or is it about something deeper?"

"What is my past trying to teach me through this moment?"

"Am I seeing this situation clearly, or through the lens of an old wound?"

Awareness is the first step. Because once you see the pattern, you can begin to break it.

Your Past Shaped You, But It Doesn't Have to Control You

You are not the same person you were when those wounds were created. You are stronger now. More aware. More capable of healing than ever before.

It is not your fault that you were hurt. But it is your responsibility to heal.

You deserve a life that is free from old pain. You deserve relationships where you feel safe. You deserve a mind that doesn't hold you hostage to past experiences.

And the best part? **Healing is possible.**

You do not have to stay stuck in the past. You can choose, right now, to begin releasing what no longer serves you.

Breaking Negative Thought Patterns—How to Stop the Spiral of Overthinking

Have you ever noticed how a single negative thought can ruin your entire day?

Maybe it starts with something small—someone doesn't text back, your boss gives you a vague response, or you remember something embarrassing from years ago. Before you know it, your mind is spiraling, creating stories, assumptions, and worst-case scenarios that may not even be real.

This is the trap of negative thought patterns.

They don't just affect your mood. They affect your energy, your confidence, and even your physical health. And if left unchecked, they can keep you trapped in cycles of stress, self-doubt, and anxiety.

But here's something that most people don't know—**your brain is not the master. You are.** And once you understand how to break these patterns, you can reclaim control over your mind.

The Science of Negative Thoughts (This Will Blow Your Mind)

Your brain is wired for survival, not happiness.

Thousands of years ago, our ancestors needed to stay alert to danger. Their brains were trained to **look for threats**—a rustling in the bushes, a strange sound, anything that signaled danger. This is why we, as humans, tend to **focus more on negative things than positive ones.**

It's called the **Negativity Bias,** and it's why:

- You remember criticism more than compliments.
- You replay awkward moments in your head long after they happen.
- You assume the worst when faced with uncertainty.

Your brain thinks it's protecting you. But in reality, it's keeping you stuck in a loop of fear-based thinking.

Here's the wild part—**the more you think a negative thought, the stronger it becomes.**

Every thought you have **creates a neural pathway in your brain.** The more you repeat a thought, the deeper that pathway gets, making it easier for your brain to default to negativity.

But the good news? **You can rewire your brain.** Just as negative thoughts create patterns, positive thoughts can break them.

Breaking Free—A Simple Exercise to Rewire Your Mind

Your thoughts are not facts. They are just **mental habits.** And like any habit, they can be changed.

Let's do a quick thought detox right now:

1. **Catch the Thought –** The next time you notice yourself spiraling, pause. Say to yourself, "Wait, what am I thinking right now?"

2. **Question It –** Ask yourself:

- Is this thought 100% true?
- Do I have real proof, or am I just assuming?
- Would I say this to a friend if they were in my situation?

3. **Flip the Thought –** Once you see the pattern, reframe it. If your thought is "I'm failing at everything," change it to "I'm learning, and I have handled tough

situations before."

4. **Interrupt the Cycle Physically –** The moment you feel caught in negative thinking, change your physical state.

- Get up and walk.
- Splash cold water on your face.
- Take deep, intentional breaths.
- Move your body.

Your brain and body are connected. **When you change your physical state, you disrupt the thought spiral.**

Your Mind is a Garden—Be Careful What You Plant

Imagine your mind is a garden. Every thought is a seed.

If you constantly plant seeds of doubt, fear, and negativity, those thoughts will grow into your reality. But if you start planting seeds of possibility, self-trust, and peace, you'll create a mental space where healing and happiness naturally grow.

You don't have to let your thoughts control you.

You are not your thoughts.

You are the observer of them.

And you have the power to change them.

Next time your mind starts spiraling, pause and remind yourself:

"I have the power to choose my thoughts. I am in control of my mind, and my mind is not in control of me."

Because the moment you take back control of your thoughts, you take back control of your life.

Why Crying is a Superpower—The Science of Healing Through Tears

Most people see crying as a sign of weakness. From a young age, we are told to "be strong," to wipe away our tears, to hide our emotions.

But what if I told you that **crying is not a weakness—it's one of the most powerful healing tools your body has?**

Tears are not just water. They carry emotions, chemical signals, and a profound ability to release pain that has been stored in your body for years. The truth is, **crying is a natural reset button for your heart, mind, and even your nervous system.**

The Science of Crying—Why It's More Powerful Than You Think

Most people assume crying is just an emotional reaction. But scientists have discovered that tears serve a much **deeper, biological** purpose.

There are three types of tears:

1. **Basal Tears** – These keep your eyes moist and protect them from dryness.

2. **Reflex Tears** – These flush out irritants, like dust or onion fumes.

3. **Emotional Tears** – These are the ones that truly heal you.

Here's where it gets interesting—**emotional tears contain stress hormones and toxins that your body needs to release.**

A study by biochemist Dr. William Frey found that emotional tears contain:

- Cortisol (the stress hormone)

- Endorphins (natural painkillers)

- Leucine-enkephalin (a natural mood booster)

When you cry, your body is literally **flushing out stress** and resetting your emotional state. This is why, after a deep cry, you often feel lighter, calmer, and more at peace.

Holding back tears, on the other hand, **traps stress inside the body**—leading to physical tension, headaches, and even long-term health issues.

Crying is **not a breakdown**—it's a breakthrough.

What Happens When You Suppress Tears?

Imagine a pressure cooker. If you keep increasing the heat without releasing steam, it will eventually explode.

Your emotions work the same way. When you suppress your tears, the emotions don't disappear. They build up, turning into:

- Anxiety and restlessness
- Physical aches, especially in the chest and throat
- Sudden emotional outbursts over small things
- Emotional numbness (where you feel nothing at all)

Tears are your body's way of **releasing** that pressure before it overwhelms you.

How to Cry in a Way That Actually Heals You

If you've been holding back tears for a long time, it might feel difficult to let go. But crying doesn't have to be random or uncontrolled. **It can be intentional, healing, and deeply transformative.**

Here's how you can make crying a healing practice:

1. **Create a Safe Space** – Find a quiet place where you won't be interrupted. This could be your bedroom, a warm shower, or even your car.

2. **Play Music That Moves You** – Sometimes, the right song unlocks emotions we've buried for too long.

3. **Give Yourself Permission** – Remind yourself: "I am safe to feel this. My body knows how to release what no longer serves me."

4. **Let the Tears Flow Naturally** – Don't hold back, but also don't force it. Allow yourself to simply be in the moment.

5. **After Crying, Take a Deep Breath** – Notice how your body feels. Most people report feeling lighter, clearer, and even more energized after a deep cry.

6. **Drink Water & Ground Yourself** – Crying releases energy, and replenishing your body helps restore balance. Place a hand on your heart and say, "I am healing."

Crying is Strength, Not Weakness

Some of the strongest people in the world cry often—not because they are weak, but because they understand the power of releasing what no longer serves them.

So the next time you feel tears coming, don't stop them.

Let them flow. Let them cleanse you.

Because every tear you shed is a step closer to healing.

And isn't that what this journey is all about?

Let's continue…

PART 2

44 WAYS TO HEAL
(Simple, Powerful, and Life-Changing Techniques)

MIND & EMOTIONAL HEALING: HEAL FROM THE INSIDE OUT

Healing a Broken Heart—Step-by-Step Guide to Moving On

Heartbreak feels like an earthquake in the soul—shaking everything you once believed was stable. It's not just about losing a person; it's about losing a version of yourself that existed with them. The pain can feel unbearable at times. It seeps into your thoughts, your body, even your dreams. But here's what most people don't tell you: heartbreak is not a sign of weakness. It is proof that you loved deeply.

And just as love can break you, love can also heal you.

This chapter isn't about quick fixes or pretending to "move on." True healing means processing, releasing, and rebuilding—so that you don't carry this pain into your future.

If you're ready, let's begin.

Step 1: Accept That Healing Comes in Waves

Heartbreak doesn't heal in a straight line. Some days you'll feel strong, other days, you'll fall apart over the smallest memory. This is normal. Healing happens in waves, and fighting against your emotions will only make them stronger.

Take a deep breath and remind yourself: "I am allowed to feel this. I am not broken. I am healing."

Transformative Exercise: The Emotional Release Journal

Write a letter to the person you lost—but do NOT send it.

In this letter, express:

- What you wish you could say to them.
- The pain you feel and why.
- What you will no longer carry in your heart.

When you're done, burn the letter or rip it into pieces. As you watch it turn to ashes, whisper to yourself:

"I release this pain. It no longer controls me."

This symbolic act helps the mind and heart process closure on a deeper level.

Step 2: Cut the Emotional Cords That Keep You Attached

Even after a breakup, an invisible bond remains. You might still feel their presence, still hear their voice in your mind, still dream about them. This is because emotional and energetic ties don't break instantly—they must be consciously released.

Transformative Exercise: The Cord-Cutting Visualization

1. Close your eyes and take deep breaths. Imagine yourself standing in front of the person you need to release.

2. Visualize a glowing cord connecting you and them—this cord represents the emotional attachment.

3. Now, imagine a golden light surrounding you, filling you with strength and peace.

4. See yourself holding a pair of energetic scissors or a sword of light.

5. Say out loud: "I release you with love. I take back my energy and return yours to you."

6. Now, cut the cord and watch it dissolve. Feel yourself becoming lighter.

This practice is powerful—it tells your subconscious mind that you are ready to let go. Repeat it whenever you feel yourself slipping back into old emotions.

Step 3: Reprogram Your Mind—The Stories You Tell Yourself Matter

Heartbreak often brings painful self-talk:

"I wasn't good enough."

"I'll never find love again."

"I wasted so much time."

None of these are true. They are emotional wounds disguised as thoughts.

The truth is: your worth is not dependent on someone else's ability to see it.

Transformative Exercise: Rewrite the Narrative

Take a piece of paper and divide it into two columns:

- **Left Column:** Write down the negative thoughts your mind is repeating.

- **Right Column:** Rewrite each one with a truth that empowers you.

- Example:

- "I wasn't enough for them." → ✓ "Their inability to love me does not define my worth."

- "I will never love again." → ✓ "Love exists in infinite forms, and I am open to receiving it."

Read your rewritten truths out loud every day until they become your new belief system.

Step 4: Rebuild the Love You Gave Away

Sometimes, heartbreak isn't just about missing the person—it's about missing the version of ourselves that existed with them.

You loved deeply. You gave freely. But now, that love has nowhere to go.

Transformative Exercise: The Mirror Ritual for Self-Love

Stand in front of a mirror. Look into your own eyes and say:

"I choose to give myself the love I once gave to others. I am whole. I am worthy. I am enough."

At first, this might feel strange. But over time, this practice rebuilds self-love and shifts your energy from lack to wholeness.

Step 5: Trust That This Pain is Clearing Space for Something Better

Right now, it may feel like love has abandoned you. But love never abandons—it only redirects.

Think of a time in your life when you thought you wouldn't survive something, but you did. You are stronger than you think.

One day, this heartbreak will be a chapter in your story—a chapter that leads you to a version of yourself that is wiser, stronger, and more radiant than ever before.

Final Exercise: The Future Self Letter

Write a letter from your healed, future self to the version of you reading this chapter today.

Your future self has already survived this. They have already found peace. What advice would they give you?

Once you write it, keep this letter in a safe place. One day, when you've healed, read it again. You'll realize that everything your future self promised came true.

Your Heart is Healing—One Step at a Time

Healing a broken heart isn't about forgetting the past. It's about making peace with it, so you can step fully into your future.

You are not broken. You are becoming whole again.

And the love you thought you lost? It's still inside you—it's just waiting for the right person, the right time, and the right version of YOU.

Take a deep breath. Let's continue.

Affirmations That Rewire Your Mind for Strength & Peace

Your mind is a powerful tool—it can either be your greatest healer or your greatest enemy.

Every thought you think sends signals to your body, your emotions, and even your energy field. And whether you realize it or not, the thoughts you repeat daily are shaping your reality.

If your mind has been filled with negativity—self-doubt, fear, worry, or limiting beliefs—it's time to reset and rewire your inner dialogue.

Affirmations aren't just "positive words" you say to yourself. They are commands to your subconscious mind. When practiced consistently, they can:

- Shift your beliefs at a deep, subconscious level.

- Heal old thought patterns that keep you stuck.

- Strengthen your emotional resilience.

- Create peace, confidence, and inner power.

But for affirmations to truly work, they must be practiced the right way. Let's go deep and transform your mind—one affirmation at a time.

The Science Behind Affirmations (This Will Blow Your Mind)

Your brain is constantly rewiring itself. This is called neuroplasticity—the ability of your brain to form new neural connections based on your thoughts and experiences.

Every time you think a thought, your brain strengthens that pathway. The more you repeat a negative thought, the stronger that belief becomes.

For example, if you've spent years telling yourself:

"I'm not good enough."

"I always fail."

"Nothing ever works out for me."

Then those thoughts have become automatic programs in your brain.

But here's the incredible part—you can change those programs. Just like a muscle grows stronger with exercise, your mind can be retrained through intentional repetition.

This is where affirmations come in.

By repeating new, empowering thoughts, you begin rewiring your brain to think differently—automatically.

Step 1: Creating Affirmations That Actually Work

Many people try affirmations but don't see results. Why? Because they use them in a way that doesn't connect with their subconscious mind.

To make affirmations powerful, follow these guidelines:

- **Make Them Present-Tense** – Your subconscious only understands the NOW. Instead of saying "I will be confident," say "I am confident."
- **Make Them Emotional** – Words without feeling have no power. Feel the truth of what you're saying.
- **Make Them Personal** – Choose affirmations that

truly resonate with you. If saying "I love myself" feels fake right now, start with "I am learning to love myself more each day."

Step 2: The 3-Minute Mind Reset

Here's a simple but powerful exercise to instantly shift your energy:

1. Find a quiet place and close your eyes. Take a deep breath in, and exhale slowly.

2. Place your hand on your heart. Feel the warmth of your own energy.

3. Say an affirmation out loud, slowly and intentionally.

- *"I am worthy of love and happiness."*
- *"I am safe, strong, and deeply supported."*
- *"I release fear and welcome peace."*

4. Repeat the affirmation three times while deeply feeling its truth.

5. Take one more deep breath and open your eyes. Notice how different you feel.

This technique rewires your subconscious quickly by using breath, voice, and physical touch to anchor the new belief.

Step 3: The Ultimate Affirmation List for Strength & Peace

Choose the affirmations that speak to your soul. Say them daily—morning, night, or whenever you need a reset.

For Confidence & Self-Worth:

- *I am more than enough, exactly as I am.*
- *I trust myself fully.*
- *I am worthy of success, love, and joy.*

- *I release the fear of what others think of me.*

For Healing & Letting Go:
- *I forgive myself and others, setting myself free.*
- *I choose to let go of what no longer serves me.*
- *I am healing, one breath at a time.*
- *My past does not define me—only my present choices do.*

For Inner Peace & Emotional Strength:
- *I am calm, centered, and at peace.*
- *No matter what happens, I choose peace over worry.*
- *I am safe. The universe supports me.*
- *I trust life's timing and allow things to unfold with ease.*

Step 4: The Mirror Technique—A Game Changer

One of the most powerful ways to practice affirmations is by saying them in front of a mirror.

Why? Because when you look into your own eyes while speaking, your subconscious absorbs the words ten times more effectively.

Mirror Exercise:
1. Stand in front of a mirror. Look into your own eyes.
2. Say an affirmation with full presence and belief.
3. If emotions arise, allow them. Healing is happening.
4. Repeat for 2 minutes daily.

This may feel uncomfortable at first, but over time, you will start to believe the words deeply—and your mind will begin to shift automatically.

Step 5: Make It a Daily Habit

The key to reprogramming your mind is consistency.

Think of affirmations like brushing your teeth—you wouldn't skip a day, right? Treat your mental and emotional health the same way.

- Set a reminder on your phone.

- Stick affirmation notes on your mirror or fridge.

- Repeat them before bed or right after waking up.

Within 30 days, you'll notice a shift. In 60 days, you'll start feeling different. In 90 days, your mind will be rewired.

Your thoughts create your reality.

Choose them wisely.

Your Mind is Transforming—One Thought at a Time

You are no longer at the mercy of old, negative beliefs.

You are now the creator of new, empowering ones.

Speak life into yourself. Choose thoughts that nourish you. And watch as your inner world—and outer reality— begin to change.

You are powerful.

You are worthy.

You are healing.

How to Rebuild Confidence After Rejection or Failure

Rejection and failure have a way of making us question everything—our worth, our abilities, and sometimes even our purpose. When something we deeply wanted does not work out, it can feel like life itself is pushing us away, telling us that we are not good enough.

But here is the truth: Rejection is not a reflection of your worth. It is a redirection.

Every successful person, every strong leader, and every wise soul has faced rejection and failure. The difference is in how they responded. They did not let it define them—they used it to rebuild themselves stronger than before.

If you are struggling to regain your confidence after a setback, this chapter will guide you through a deep, transformative process to rebuild your self-worth and move forward with strength.

Step 1: Separate the Event from Your Identity

One of the biggest mistakes people make after rejection or failure is internalizing it. They do not just see it as something that happened; they see it as proof that they are not good enough.

Take a moment to reflect:

- Did you fail, or did a plan not work out as expected?
- Were you rejected, or was it simply not the right fit?
- Is this setback permanent, or is it just a moment in time?

Your worth has not changed. Your value is not determined by someone else's inability to see it. Rejection does not mean you are unworthy; it means you are being redirected toward something better suited for you.

Step 2: Reframe the Meaning of Failure

Society has conditioned us to believe that failure is something to avoid. But what if failure is actually a sign that you are growing?

Every time you fail, you are learning. Every time you are rejected, you are getting closer to where you are meant to be. Consider these examples:

- Thomas Edison failed over a thousand times before inventing the lightbulb.

- J.K. Rowling was rejected by multiple publishers before Harry Potter became a global phenomenon.
- Oprah Winfrey was told she was "not fit for television" before becoming one of the most influential people in media.

If they had given up after rejection, the world would have never seen their greatness. The same applies to you. Your current setback is just one chapter—not your entire story.

Step 3: Identify the Hidden Lesson

Every rejection carries a lesson. Sometimes, we are too hurt to see it, but it is always there.

Take a moment to reflect:

- What can you learn from this experience?
- Did this rejection reveal something you need to improve or change?
- Did it protect you from something that was not truly meant for you?

Write down your insights. The faster you extract the lesson, the faster you can move forward with clarity and wisdom.

Step 4: Rebuild Your Inner Confidence

Confidence is not about never failing—it is about trusting yourself enough to rise again. The strongest confidence comes from within, not from external validation.

Try this daily self-affirmation exercise to rebuild your self-belief:

1. Stand in front of a mirror.
2. Look into your own eyes and say out loud:
- "I am capable, regardless of this setback."

- "My worth is not defined by this moment."
- "I choose to keep moving forward with confidence."
3. Repeat this daily for the next 30 days and notice the shift in your mindset.

Your mind believes what you tell it repeatedly. Replace self-doubt with self-trust.

Step 5: Take Small, Bold Actions

One of the quickest ways to regain confidence is through small wins. After rejection or failure, fear can make you hesitant to try again. The solution is to take small steps that rebuild your momentum.

- If you were rejected from a job, apply for another today.
- If you failed at a project, take a small step toward improving it.
- If someone walked away from you, invest time in self-growth and new connections.

Do not wait until you feel "ready." Confidence is built through action, not overthinking.

Step 6: Trust the Bigger Picture

Sometimes, rejection is protection. Sometimes, failure is the first step toward something far greater.

Think about a time in your life when something did not work out—but later, you realized it was for the best. The same might be happening now.

You may not see it yet, but trust that this experience is shaping you into the person you are meant to become. The path may not be clear now, but if you keep moving forward, one day, you will look back and understand exactly why this had to happen.

You are not defined by this moment. You are stronger than you think.

Take a deep breath, stand tall, and move forward with confidence.

Let us continue.

The Art of Forgiveness—A Simple Practice That Sets You Free

Forgiveness is one of the most misunderstood aspects of healing. Many believe it means excusing someone's behavior, forgetting the past, or allowing the same pain to happen again. But real forgiveness is none of these things.

True forgiveness is not about them—it is about you. It is the act of releasing the emotional weight that keeps you tied to a past that no longer serves you. It is an inner decision to set yourself free from the burden of anger, resentment, and pain.

Holding onto anger can feel like power, but in reality, it drains you. The pain you carry does not punish the other person—it only poisons your own heart, mind, and energy. Forgiveness is not weakness. It is an act of reclaiming your peace.

There was once a man who spent decades resenting his father. As a child, he had felt abandoned, unseen, and unloved. That pain shaped his entire life—his relationships, his career, even the way he saw himself. The anger gave him purpose at first, but over time, it turned into exhaustion. He carried his father's absence everywhere he went, allowing it to define his story. It was not until he chose to release that anger that he realized something powerful: his father had stopped hurting him years ago, but he had been hurting himself every single day since.

This is what happens when we refuse to forgive. We chain ourselves to the very thing we want freedom from.

Forgiveness does not mean forgetting. It does not mean letting the same situation happen again. It means choosing yourself over your pain.

The Healing Practice of Letting Go

If there is someone you are struggling to forgive, consider this: they may never apologize, and they may never understand the depth of what they did. But your healing is not dependent on them. It is a gift only you can give yourself.

One of the most profound forgiveness practices comes from the ancient Hawaiian tradition of Ho'oponopono. This simple yet powerful method allows you to release pain while restoring inner peace.

To practice it, take a deep breath, close your eyes, and bring to mind the person or situation that has caused you pain. As you hold this image, repeat these four phrases:

"I am sorry."

"Please forgive me."

"Thank you."

"I love you."

At first, this may feel difficult, even impossible. The words may feel forced, and resistance may rise. That is part of the process. Forgiveness is not a one-time decision; it is a practice. Over time, as you continue, the energy of resentment begins to dissolve, and you feel the weight lifting.

Some people resist forgiveness because they believe it means giving up their boundaries. But forgiveness and boundaries go hand in hand. You can release anger and still choose to protect your peace. You can forgive someone and still decide they have no place in your life. The difference is that now, your decision comes from clarity rather than pain.

Forgiveness is not about changing the past. It is about changing your relationship with it. The past cannot be rewritten, but it can lose its grip on you.

If you have been carrying pain, resentment, or anger, ask yourself: *Is this weight helping me, or is it holding me back?* The answer is already within you.

Now is the time to release. Now is the time to heal.

Take a deep breath, and let go.

How Visualization Can Heal Your Pain & Manifest a Better Life

Your mind is a powerful force. It can keep you trapped in pain, or it can be the key to your deepest healing. What you see in your mind shapes what you experience in your reality. If your inner world is filled with memories of the past, self-doubt, or fear, your outer world will reflect that. But if you learn to harness the power of visualization, you can begin to rewire your mind, heal emotional wounds, and shape the life you truly want.

Many think of visualization as simply daydreaming, but it is much more than that. Scientific studies have shown that the brain cannot distinguish between what is real and what is vividly imagined. When you visualize something with intensity and belief, your brain fires the same neurons as if you were actually experiencing it. Athletes use visualization to enhance their performance. Surgeons use it to sharpen their skills. Healers use it to shift their energy and open themselves to transformation.

The question is, how can you use visualization to heal?

The Deep Healing Visualization Method

If you have been carrying emotional pain, this practice will help you release it from your mind and body.

Find a quiet place where you will not be disturbed. Sit comfortably, close your eyes, and take a deep breath. Let yourself sink into stillness.

Now, bring to mind the pain you wish to release. It could be heartbreak, fear, trauma, or self-doubt. Do not run from it—simply acknowledge that it is there.

Imagine this pain as a dark, heavy energy inside you. Where does it sit in your body? Your chest? Your stomach? Your shoulders? Observe it without judgment.

Now, visualize a warm, golden light appearing above you. This light is pure healing energy. As it descends, feel it touch the top of your head, then slowly move down, filling you with warmth and peace.

See this light gently dissolving the dark energy inside you, replacing it with strength, love, and clarity. Imagine yourself feeling lighter, freer, as if the burden has finally been lifted.

Now, picture the best version of yourself—the version that has fully healed, the one who is confident, at peace, and unburdened by the past. See yourself smiling, standing tall, moving through life with ease.

Breathe deeply and step into that version of yourself. Feel the shift. This is not just a fantasy—this is your future reality. The more you visualize it, the more it becomes imprinted in your subconscious, guiding your actions, thoughts, and emotions toward healing.

When you are ready, slowly open your eyes. Take a moment to notice the calmness in your body. The shift has already begun.

Why This Works

Your subconscious mind does not respond to logic—it responds to images, emotions, and repetition. The more you practice this, the more your brain will begin to believe in your healing. And once your mind believes it, your body and energy will follow.

This practice is not about escaping reality. It is about creating a new reality—one where you are no longer defined by past pain but by the strength you have cultivated within.

Healing does not happen outside of you. It happens within. And with every visualization, you are reminding yourself that healing is not just possible—it is already unfolding.

Take another deep breath. You are becoming the person you were always meant to be.

The Dustbin Method—A Trick to Instantly Let Go of Negative Thoughts

The mind is like a house. Over the years, it collects things—memories, beliefs, emotions, and thoughts. Some of these thoughts are useful, but many are just clutter, taking up space and making it difficult to feel at peace. Negative thoughts, especially the ones we replay over and over, act like old junk that should have been thrown out long ago. Yet, we hold onto them, sometimes without even realizing it.

Letting go is not just about telling yourself to "think positive." It is about releasing the mental weight that is keeping you stuck. If you have ever struggled with overthinking, worry, or thoughts that seem impossible to silence, the Dustbin Method is a simple but powerful way to clear them out of your mind.

How the Dustbin Method Works

Your mind responds strongly to visual metaphors. The Dustbin Method works by using a mental image that signals to your subconscious that it is time to release what no longer serves you. It is a simple yet effective exercise that allows you to remove toxic thoughts, self-doubt, and emotional baggage in just a few minutes.

Step 1: Identify the Thought That Needs to Go

Pause for a moment and notice what thought is bothering you. Is it a fear? A regret? A painful memory? Do not suppress it—simply acknowledge it.

Step 2: Create a Mental Dustbin

Close your eyes and take a deep breath. Now, imagine a large dustbin in front of you. It can be any size or color—whatever feels right to you. This is your personal space for clearing negativity.

Step 3: Throw the Thought Away

Visualize taking the unwanted thought and crumpling it like a piece of paper. See yourself physically tossing it into the dustbin. As you do this, say silently or out loud:

"I no longer need this thought. I release it now."

Feel the relief as you let it go.

Step 4: Seal the Dustbin

Imagine closing the lid of the dustbin. You can even visualize locking it or tying it shut. Know that what is inside no longer has control over you. It has been discarded, just like old trash.

Step 5: Empty the Dustbin

Now, picture the dustbin being taken away—far away from you, disappearing into the distance. As it goes, feel the space in your mind becoming lighter, clearer, and more open.

When you are ready, open your eyes. Notice how you feel. The thought may try to return, but remember—you have already thrown it away. There is no need to pick it back up.

Why This Works

Your brain treats visualization as reality. By physically imagining yourself discarding a thought, your subconscious registers it as "gone." The more you practice this, the easier it becomes to stop overthinking and move on from mental clutter.

Negative thoughts lose their power when you stop holding onto them. The Dustbin Method is a simple yet powerful way to remind yourself that you are in control of your mind, not the other way around.

Whenever you find yourself stuck in an endless loop of worry or negativity, pause and repeat this process. Each time you do, you are strengthening your ability to let go.

Take a deep breath. Your mind is now lighter, clearer, and free.

Breaking Free from Perfectionism—Stop the Self-Sabotage

Perfectionism may seem like a strength. It pushes you to work harder, aim higher, and achieve more. But beneath the surface, perfectionism is not about excellence—it is about fear. The fear of making mistakes. The fear of being judged. The fear of not being enough.

Many people believe that being a perfectionist means they have high standards, but true high standards come from confidence. Perfectionism, on the other hand, comes from self-doubt. It keeps you trapped in endless cycles of overthinking, procrastination, and self-criticism, never allowing you to truly feel at peace with yourself.

If you are constantly feeling exhausted, anxious, or never satisfied with your own efforts, it is time to break free.

Why Perfectionism is Holding You Back

Perfectionism does not protect you—it limits you. The more you chase flawlessness, the more you fear failure, which leads to hesitation, procrastination, and sometimes, complete avoidance of the things that matter most.

Imagine a writer who wants to publish a book but is afraid that it will not be perfect. They keep rewriting the first chapter over and over, never making progress. Or an artist who never shares their work because they are afraid it is not good enough. This cycle repeats itself in careers, relationships, and personal growth.

Perfectionism convinces you that "not ready" is a valid excuse, but the truth is, no one ever feels fully ready. Growth happens in action, not in waiting.

The Perfectionism Release Exercise

If perfectionism has been holding you back, it is time to retrain your mind. This exercise will help you shift from the impossible expectation of "perfect" to the powerful mindset of "progress."

Step 1: Name the Fear

Think about an area of your life where perfectionism is keeping you stuck. It could be work, relationships, creative projects, or even self-image. Write it down.

Now, ask yourself: What am I really afraid of?

- Are you afraid of failure?
- Are you afraid of judgment?
- Are you afraid of disappointing yourself or others?

Acknowledging the fear is the first step to releasing its hold over you.

Step 2: Lower the Stakes

Perfectionism makes every decision feel like life or death. But in reality, most things are not as high-stakes as they seem.

Take the thing you have been avoiding and ask: What is the worst that could happen if it is not perfect?

Will people stop loving you? Will your life fall apart? Or will you simply learn and grow from the experience? Most of the time, our fears are far greater in our minds than in reality.

Step 3: Set a "Good Enough" Goal

Instead of aiming for perfection, aim for completion.

- If you have been avoiding writing, commit to writing for just 10 minutes.

- If you have been afraid to post your work, share something small today.

- If you hesitate to speak up, set a goal to express one opinion this week.

Perfectionists often believe that success comes from doing things flawlessly, but in reality, success comes from showing up consistently.

Step 4: Challenge Your Inner Critic

Perfectionism thrives on self-judgment. It tells you that you are not good enough, that your work is not ready, that you should wait until you are better. But here is something important to remember: the voice of perfectionism is not the voice of truth—it is the voice of fear.

The next time you catch yourself thinking, *"This is not good enough,"* or *"I am not ready,"* replace it with:

"This is a work in progress, and that is enough."

"I am growing, and growth is more important than perfection."

"I would rather start imperfectly than never start at all."

Each time you correct your inner dialogue, you weaken the grip of perfectionism.

Living a Life Free from Perfectionism

Perfectionism keeps you in the illusion of control, but true freedom comes when you realize that life is meant to be messy, evolving, and imperfect.

Think of nature. Flowers bloom with asymmetry. Rivers flow in unpredictable directions. Even the sky is constantly shifting. Yet, everything is perfectly as it is meant to be. The same applies to you.

Let go of the belief that you need to be perfect to be worthy. You are already enough, exactly as you are.

Release the pressure. Start where you are. Let go of the need for perfect outcomes and focus on taking small, consistent steps.

The more you embrace imperfection, the more you will realize that life is not about doing everything flawlessly—it is about experiencing it fully.

Now, take a deep breath. You are free.

Inner Child Healing—Heal the Younger You That Still Hurts

There is a part of you that still remembers. The child within you—the one who once felt joy without fear, the one who trusted without hesitation, the one who loved without conditions—still exists. But so does the child who felt abandoned, rejected, unheard, or not good enough.

Many of the emotional struggles we face as adults—self-doubt, fear of rejection, feelings of unworthiness—are not just random patterns. They are echoes of childhood wounds that were never fully healed.

Inner child healing is not about blaming the past. It is about acknowledging the parts of you that were hurt and giving them the love they never received.

If you have ever wondered why certain triggers hit so deeply or why the same emotional patterns repeat in your life, it is time to meet, understand, and heal your inner child.

Recognizing the Wounds of Your Inner Child

Your childhood experiences shape your belief systems, your relationships, and even the way you see yourself. Some wounds are obvious, but others are subtle, woven into your subconscious mind.

Do you ever:

- Struggle with people-pleasing, always seeking approval?
- Feel deep self-doubt or fear of failure?
- Have a hard time setting boundaries, fearing rejection?
- Feel unworthy of love or success?
- Experience sudden emotional reactions that seem disproportionate to the situation?

These are often signs that your inner child is still carrying unprocessed pain.

The first step to healing is awareness. Ask yourself: What did I need as a child that I never fully received? Love? Safety? Validation? Freedom to express yourself?

This question will open the door to deep healing.

The Inner Child Connection Exercise

Healing your inner child means reconnecting with them—speaking to them, comforting them, and letting them know they are safe now.

Find a quiet space where you can be undisturbed. Close your eyes, take a deep breath, and imagine yourself traveling back in time. Visualize yourself as a child—perhaps at an age when you felt hurt, alone, or misunderstood.

See them standing before you. Observe their expression, their emotions, the energy they carry. Now, gently kneel down and look into their eyes.

Speak to them with kindness. Say:

"I see you. I hear you. I know you have been carrying this pain for a long time. But you are safe now. You are loved. You are enough."

If emotions rise, let them flow. You are not just imagining this—you are reconnecting with a part of yourself that has been waiting to be acknowledged.

When you feel ready, take your inner child's hand and walk with them. Show them a safe place—whether it is a beautiful garden, a glowing room, or simply your present self's loving embrace. Let them know they are no longer alone.

Before ending the exercise, promise them that you will listen to them from now on, that you will not abandon them the way they once felt abandoned.

Take a deep breath and slowly open your eyes. Notice the warmth in your heart. The healing has begun.

Reparenting Yourself—Becoming the Adult You Needed

Now that you have met your inner child, the next step is reparenting yourself—giving yourself the love, protection, and guidance that you once longed for.

- If you needed encouragement as a child, start speaking to yourself with kindness.
- If you need safety, set strong boundaries and honor your needs.

- If you need to be seen and heard, express yourself freely, without fear.

Every time you choose self-love over self-criticism, you are healing your inner child. Every time you listen to your emotions instead of suppressing them, you are showing them that they matter.

Healing does not happen in one moment. It is a process of showing up for yourself, day after day.

You are not just healing the past—you are transforming your future.

Take another deep breath. You are safe now.

ENERGY & SPIRITUAL HEALING: CLEAR BLOCKS & RAISE YOUR VIBRATION

Crystals for Healing—How to Use Amethyst, Rose Quartz & More

Since ancient times, crystals have been used as tools for healing, balance, and spiritual transformation. Civilizations from Egypt to India, Greece to China, have believed that certain stones hold vibrational frequencies that can align with our own energy fields, helping us heal, protect, and strengthen different aspects of our lives.

Crystals are not magic. They do not instantly fix problems. But they do act as **energy conductors**, amplifying your intentions, supporting emotional healing, and creating a sense of balance within you. If you have ever felt drawn to a particular crystal without knowing why, it is likely that your energy was instinctively seeking what it needed.

Healing with crystals is about more than just carrying a stone—it is about **intention, connection, and allowing yourself to receive their support.**

Choosing the Right Crystal for Your Healing Journey

Different crystals support different types of healing. If you are new to working with them, start with what you intuitively feel drawn to. Here are some of the most powerful crystals for emotional and spiritual healing:

- **Amethyst** – A deeply calming stone that helps with emotional balance, anxiety relief, and spiritual clarity.

- **Rose Quartz** – Known as the "stone of unconditional love," it heals heartbreak, promotes self-love, and restores trust in relationships.

- **Black Tourmaline** – A strong protector against negativity, shielding your energy from toxic influences.

- **Clear Quartz** – A master healer that amplifies any intention, supporting physical, emotional, and mental clarity.

- **Lapis Lazuli** – A stone of truth and wisdom, helping with communication and self-expression.

The best way to choose a crystal is not by its description but by **how it makes you feel.** Hold different stones in your hand, close your eyes, and notice any sensations. Your body will guide you to what it needs.

Cleansing & Charging Your Crystals

Just like people absorb energy from their surroundings, so do crystals. Before using them for healing, they must be cleansed and charged.

Cleansing Methods:

- **Running Water** – Hold the crystal under cool, flowing water, imagining negativity washing away.

- **Smudging** – Use sage, palo santo, or incense to cleanse the crystal's energy.

- **Moonlight** – Place your crystals under the full moon to reset their vibrations.

Once cleansed, hold the crystal in your hands, set an intention, and visualize its energy supporting you.

Crystal Healing Meditation

To truly connect with your crystal, try this simple meditation:

1. Find a quiet space and hold your chosen crystal in your hands.

2. Close your eyes and take slow, deep breaths, feeling its energy in your palms.

3. Set an intention—whether it is healing, protection, or clarity—by silently affirming:

"I allow this crystal's energy to support my healing process."

4. Imagine its energy merging with yours, creating a protective and healing light around you.

5. Stay in this state for a few moments, allowing any emotions or insights to arise naturally.

When you are finished, thank the crystal and carry it with you, keeping its energy close as you move through your day.

Using Crystals in Daily Life

Crystals are most effective when they are part of your daily routine. You can:

- Wear them as jewelry to keep their energy close.

- Place them under your pillow for emotional healing while you sleep.

- Keep them at your workspace to maintain focus and clarity.

- Hold them in your palm when feeling anxious or unsettled.

The more you work with your crystals, the more attuned you become to their energy. They are not meant to replace personal effort but to **support and strengthen your healing journey.**

Take a deep breath. You are aligning with the energy that serves your highest good.

The Healing Power of Reiki—Recharge Your Mind, Body & Soul

Energy is the foundation of everything. Every thought, emotion, and physical sensation you experience is connected to the unseen energy flowing through your body. When this energy moves freely, you feel balanced, light, and at peace.

But when it is blocked—due to stress, emotional trauma, or negative experiences—you may feel stuck, anxious, or physically unwell.

Reiki is a powerful energy healing practice that helps **clear these energy blockages, recharge your body, and restore harmony to your mind and soul.** It works by channeling universal life force energy, helping to remove stagnant emotions and bring deep relaxation, inner clarity, and healing.

Many people assume that Reiki is something only trained practitioners can perform, but in reality, **anyone can tap into this healing energy.** You do not need to be spiritually gifted or have years of experience. You only need an open heart and the willingness to receive.

Understanding Reiki Energy & How It Works

The word "Reiki" comes from two Japanese words:

- **Rei** – meaning "universal life force"
- **Ki** – meaning "energy"

Reiki is based on the idea that energy flows through all living things. When this energy is high, you feel healthy, positive, and full of life. When it is low, you feel drained, anxious, or unwell.

A Reiki session works by channeling this healing energy through light touch or even from a distance. Practitioners often place their hands over different energy points in the body, allowing the flow of Reiki to cleanse and balance the system.

The beauty of Reiki is that **it does not require belief to work.** Whether you are deeply spiritual or simply curious, Reiki energy will move where it is needed, helping to release what no longer serves you.

Self-Reiki: A Simple Practice to Heal Yourself

Reiki is not just something you receive from others—you can also use it to heal yourself. Here is a simple self-Reiki practice to restore balance and calmness:

1. **Find a quiet space and sit comfortably.** Close your eyes and take a few deep breaths.

2. **Set an intention for your healing.** Silently affirm, *"I welcome healing energy into my body and mind."*

3. **Place your hands over your heart.** Feel the warmth of your own touch. Imagine soft, golden light filling your chest, dissolving any heaviness or sadness.

4. **Move your hands to different areas of your body.** You can place them on your stomach (for emotional balance), forehead (for mental clarity), or anywhere you feel tension. Allow the warmth to soothe you.

5. **Breathe deeply and visualize energy flowing through you.** Imagine any negativity melting away, leaving you lighter and more at peace.

Even five minutes of self-Reiki can create a noticeable shift in your energy, reducing stress and restoring inner calm.

How Reiki Helps with Emotional & Physical Healing

Many people turn to Reiki when they feel emotionally overwhelmed or physically exhausted. It is known to:

- **Reduce stress and anxiety** by calming the nervous system.

- **Release stored emotional pain** that has been buried in the body.

- **Improve sleep and relaxation** by bringing the body into a deep state of peace.

- **Strengthen the immune system** by balancing the body's natural energy flow.

The effects of Reiki are subtle yet profound. Some feel an immediate sense of lightness, while for others, the healing unfolds gradually. It is not about forcing change, but rather **allowing the body to return to its natural state of balance.**

Receiving Reiki from a Distance

One of the most fascinating aspects of Reiki is that it does not require physical touch. Distance Reiki allows healing energy to be sent across space and time, making it just as effective as in-person sessions.

If you ever feel emotionally drained or need support but cannot access a healer, simply take a moment to invite Reiki energy into your space. Close your eyes and affirm:

"I am open to receiving healing energy for my highest good."

Many report feeling warmth, tingling sensations, or deep relaxation after receiving distance Reiki. This reminds us that healing is not confined to physical limits—**it moves where it is needed.**

Embracing Reiki as a Healing Tool

Reiki is not about fixing something that is broken—it is about **returning to wholeness.** Whether you choose to practice self-Reiki or receive it from a healer, the experience is a gentle yet powerful reminder that you are supported, guided, and capable of deep transformation.

Healing does not have to be complicated. Sometimes, all it takes is the willingness to slow down, breathe, and allow energy to flow.

Take a moment now. Place your hands over your heart. Feel the warmth, the stillness, the life force within you. You are already healing.

Energy Cleansing Rituals—Smudging, Salt Baths & Sacred Incense

Energy is everywhere. It lingers in spaces, attaches to objects, and settles into your body, affecting your mood, emotions, and overall well-being. Have you ever walked into a room and immediately felt heavy or uneasy? Or perhaps you have experienced unexplained exhaustion after interacting with certain people? This is the result of **energy accumulation.**

Just as we shower to cleanse our physical bodies, we must also cleanse our **energetic field.** Negative energy, stress, and emotional burdens build up over time, creating blockages that can leave us feeling tired, anxious, or disconnected.

Energy cleansing rituals are powerful yet simple ways to **reset your aura, release negativity, and restore harmony—** both within yourself and in your surroundings. Let us explore how you can use smudging, salt baths, and sacred incense to purify your energy.

The Ancient Practice of Smudging

Smudging is one of the oldest spiritual cleansing techniques, used by indigenous cultures for centuries. It involves burning sacred herbs, such as sage or palo santo, to clear stagnant energy.

How to Smudge Yourself & Your Space

1. **Choose your cleansing herb.** White sage is known for deep purification, while palo santo brings uplifting, peaceful energy. You may also use cedar, lavender, or frankincense.

2. **Light the smudge stick or incense and let it smolder.** Hold a fireproof bowl underneath to catch ashes.

3. **Move the smoke around your body.** Start at your feet and work your way up, imagining all heavy energy

dissolving into the smoke.

4. **Cleanse your space.** Walk through your home, waving the smoke into corners, doorways, and windows. As you do this, set the intention:

"I release all my stagnant energy. This space is now filled with light and peace."

5. **Extinguish the smudge stick in sand or a bowl of salt.** Never leave it burning unattended.

You will immediately feel a shift—a sense of **lightness, clarity, and renewal.**

Salt Baths—Purification Through Water

Water is a natural energy cleanser, and when combined with salt, it becomes a **powerful tool for emotional and spiritual detox.** Salt absorbs negativity, clears energy blockages, and restores balance to your aura.

How to Take a Cleansing Salt Bath

1. Fill a bathtub with warm water. If you do not have a tub, you can use a bucket for a **salt foot soak.**

2. Add **one to two cups of sea salt, Himalayan salt, or Epsom salt.** These minerals draw out toxins and cleanse your energy field.

3. Optionally, add **essential oils** (lavender for relaxation, eucalyptus for clearing, or rosemary for spiritual strength).

4. Sit in the water for at least 15 minutes. As you soak, visualize stress and negativity dissolving into the water.

5. When you are finished, drain the water and imagine all unwanted energy flowing away with it.

This ritual is especially helpful after **stressful interactions, emotional turmoil, or when you feel energetically "heavy."**

Sacred Incense & Aromatic Energy Shifts

Burning incense has been used for thousands of years in temples, meditation spaces, and homes to **elevate the energy of a space and create a peaceful atmosphere.** Different incenses hold different vibrations:

- **Frankincense** – Raises spiritual energy and brings clarity.

- **Myrrh** – Grounds and stabilizes emotions.

- **Sandalwood** – Aids in deep meditation and inner peace.

- **Cinnamon** – Invites warmth, love, and prosperity.

To cleanse your space with incense, simply **light it and let the smoke drift naturally.** You can also place incense near your altar, workspace, or any area where you want to maintain positive energy.

When to Perform Energy Cleansing Rituals

Energy cleansing is not just for special occasions—it is a regular practice of self-care. Consider doing these rituals:

- **After an emotionally draining conversation or argument**

- **Before starting a new project or phase in life**

- **After coming home from crowded places or work**

- **During a full moon to release old energy**

- **Anytime you feel heavy, unfocused, or unmotivated**

Your energy is like a garden—when you tend to it, it **flourishes.**

Embracing Energy Cleansing as a Lifestyle

These rituals are not just about removing negative energy; they are about creating space for joy, clarity, and peace. The more you cleanse, the more sensitive you will become to the energy around you, learning to recognize when your spirit needs restoration.

Right now, take a deep breath. Imagine all the weight you have been carrying dissolving into the air. With every breath, you are becoming lighter, clearer, and more aligned with your true self.

Let us continue.

Cleansing Your Aura—Simple Daily Rituals for Protection & Peace

Your aura is an invisible field of energy that surrounds you, constantly interacting with the world. Just like a sponge absorbs water, your aura absorbs energy—from places, people, and experiences. This is why you sometimes feel drained after being around certain individuals or why a sudden shift in your environment can affect your mood.

A clear, vibrant aura makes you feel energized, emotionally balanced, and at peace. A cluttered or heavy aura, however, can leave you feeling sluggish, anxious, or burdened by emotions that are not even yours.

Cleansing your aura regularly is **not just a spiritual practice—it is essential for emotional and mental well-being.** When your aura is clear, you move through life with greater clarity, confidence, and protection from negativity.

How to Know When Your Aura Needs Cleansing

If your aura is congested or carrying unwanted energy, you may notice:

- A constant feeling of fatigue, even after resting.
- Increased irritability or unexplained mood swings.
- Feeling "off" after being in crowded places or emotionally charged environments.
- Struggles with focus, as if your mind is cluttered.

- A tendency to absorb others' emotions too easily.

These are signs that it is time to reset your energy field.

Simple Daily Practices to Cleanse Your Aura

Cleansing your aura does not have to be complicated. Small, consistent actions can help you maintain a **strong, vibrant, and protected energy field.**

1. Water Purification

Water is one of the most powerful natural cleansers. Taking a simple shower with **intentional awareness** can cleanse your aura. As the water flows over you, visualize it washing away all unwanted energy. You can silently affirm:

"I release all that does not serve me. I am refreshed, restored, and renewed."

For a deeper cleanse, add **sea salt or Epsom salt** to your bath. Salt has long been used to dissolve negative energy and restore balance.

2. Smudging with Sacred Herbs

Using sage, palo santo, or frankincense, lightly waft the smoke around your body, from head to toe. Imagine the smoke carrying away any heavy or stagnant energy, leaving your aura clear and radiant.

If you cannot use smoke, **essential oils like lavender or frankincense** can be applied to your pulse points for a similar effect.

3. Sun & Nature Absorption

Spending even a few minutes in **natural sunlight** helps recharge and purify your aura. Stand outside, close your eyes, and visualize golden sunlight filling your entire energy field, dissolving all heaviness and restoring vitality.

Walking barefoot on grass, touching a tree, or simply breathing fresh air can help reconnect your aura to **natural,** high-frequency energy.

4. The Aura Combing Technique

This is a simple yet effective way to remove energetic blockages.

- Stand still, take a deep breath, and imagine your aura extending about two feet around you.

- Using your hands, make sweeping motions around your body, as if you are brushing away unseen dust. Start from your head and work downward.

- As you do this, mentally affirm: "I cleanse and restore my energy. I release all that is not mine."

This quick practice can be done anytime you feel drained or out of balance.

5. Protective Shield Visualization

Once your aura is cleansed, it is important to protect it. Before starting your day, close your eyes and visualize a radiant **bubble of light surrounding you**. This shield can be golden, white, or violet—whatever color feels protective to you.

Silently affirm: *"I am surrounded by pure light. Only love and positivity can enter my space."*

This practice strengthens your energetic boundaries, preventing unwanted influences from affecting you.

Making Aura Cleansing a Daily Habit

Your energy is **as important as your physical body**. Just as you would not go days without showering, your aura needs regular cleansing to stay vibrant and healthy.

By incorporating even one of these rituals into your daily routine, you will notice a shift—**feeling lighter, clearer, and more in control of your emotional state.**

Take a moment now. Close your eyes, take a deep breath, and visualize your energy field expanding—pure, radiant, and untouchable by negativity.

You are energetically free.

Cord Cutting—How to Break Free from Toxic Relationships

Not all attachments are meant to last forever. Some connections serve their purpose and then become emotional weights, holding you back from growth, peace, and clarity.

You may have experienced relationships that drained your energy, whether with a partner, friend, colleague, or even a family member. Even after physically distancing yourself, you might find that their presence lingers in your mind, influencing your emotions and energy. This is because **energetic cords still exist between you and them.**

Cord cutting is a powerful technique that helps you **release unhealthy attachments, reclaim your energy, and move forward without emotional baggage.**

It is not about hatred, revenge, or wishing harm upon someone. It is about setting yourself free from emotional entanglements that no longer serve your highest good.

How to Know If You Need to Cut a Cord

Not every relationship requires cord cutting, but if you feel emotionally bound to someone despite knowing the connection is unhealthy, it may be time to release it.

Signs you need to cut energetic cords:

- You keep replaying conversations or past experiences with someone.
- Thinking about them drains you, even if they are no longer in your life.

- You feel their energy, emotions, or presence even when they are not around.
- The relationship was toxic, manipulative, or emotionally exhausting.
- You have tried moving on, but something still holds you back.

If any of these resonate, it means that **your energy is still entangled with theirs.** It is time to release the cord.

The Cord Cutting Ritual

This practice allows you to **sever unhealthy energetic** ties while honoring the lessons you have learned from the connection.

Step 1: Find a Quiet, Safe Space

Sit in a comfortable position, close your eyes, and take a few deep breaths. Let your body relax.

Step 2: Visualize the Cord

Imagine the person you need to detach from standing before you. See a glowing cord connecting your body to theirs. This cord represents the emotional, mental, and energetic bond that still exists between you.

Notice where the cord is attached—your heart, stomach, throat, or another area. The location often reflects the type of connection you had (for example, heart cords represent emotional ties, while cords at the stomach reflect control or fear).

Step 3: Acknowledge & Thank the Connection

Before cutting the cord, take a moment to acknowledge what this person or relationship has taught you. Even painful relationships come with lessons.

Silently or out loud, say:

"I honor the role you played in my life. I acknowledge the lessons learned. But I now release this connection with love and peace."

Step 4: Cut the Cord

Visualize a golden sword, scissors, or a beam of light appearing in your hands. With intention, cut the cord, watching it dissolve into pure light.

As you do this, affirm:

"I take back my energy. I am free. I am whole."

Feel the space where the cord was, now filled with **pure, healing light.**

Step 5: Ground & Protect Your Energy

Take a deep breath and imagine yourself surrounded by a protective sphere of light, shielding you from any lingering attachments.

Place your hand on your heart and say:

"I am no longer tied to the past. I am at peace with this release."

Slowly open your eyes. The process is complete.

What Happens After Cord Cutting?

After this ritual, you may feel **immediate relief, emotional lightness, or even deep emotional release.** Old memories or emotions may surface in the days following, but this is simply the final release of stored energy.

If you find yourself thinking about the person again, remind yourself: **"The cord is cut. I am free."**

The Power of Emotional Freedom

Letting go doesn't mean forgetting. It means choosing yourself over the weight of the past.

Every time you release an attachment that no longer serves you, you create **space for something new, something healthier, something aligned with your highest self.**

Right now, take a deep breath. Feel the freedom in your heart. You have released what was holding you back.

You are no longer bound to the past.

Karmic Blocks—Are Your Past Energies Holding You Back?

Sometimes, no matter how hard you try, it feels as if an invisible force is keeping you stuck. You repeat the same mistakes in relationships, face constant struggles with money, or feel weighed down by patterns you cannot seem to break.

This may not be just coincidence or bad luck. It may be a **karmic block**—an unresolved energy from past experiences, whether in this life or previous ones, that continues to influence your present.

Karma is not punishment; it is simply **unfinished energy seeking resolution.** When you become aware of karmic blocks, you gain the power to clear them, break old cycles, and move forward with clarity and freedom.

How Karmic Blocks Are Formed

Every action, thought, and emotion carries energy. When experiences remain unresolved—whether through guilt, resentment, or pain—this energy stays with you, shaping future events until it is acknowledged and released.

Some karmic patterns come from **this lifetime**—childhood wounds, unprocessed emotions, or painful relationships that left a deep imprint. Others may be inherited from **family karma**—patterns passed down through generations. And some may even come from **past lifetimes,** affecting your soul's journey across time.

Signs you may have a karmic block include:

- Feeling stuck in repetitive situations despite wanting change.

- Attracting the same type of toxic relationships.

- Struggling with self-worth, money, or career in ways that seem beyond logical explanation.

- Unexplainable fears or anxieties that do not seem connected to your current life experiences.

Karmic blocks are not meant to be burdens; they are opportunities for healing. Once you recognize them, you can begin the process of release.

The Karmic Release Exercise

If you sense a karmic block in your life, use this guided practice to acknowledge and clear the energy:

Step 1: Identify the Pattern

Close your eyes and reflect on an area of life where you feel stuck. Ask yourself:

- What situations keep repeating in my life?

- What emotions am I carrying that seem to hold me back?

- Do I feel an unexplained heaviness around a particular issue?

Allow your intuition to bring clarity.

Step 2: Find the Root Cause

If a specific memory or experience arises, do not push it away. Instead, observe it with curiosity. It may be something from childhood, a past relationship, or even a feeling that has been with you for as long as you can remember.

Ask yourself:

- What lesson is this experience trying to teach me?
- Am I holding onto blame, guilt, or resentment?
- What belief about myself did this situation create?

The goal isn't to relieve pain but to **bring awareness to what needs healing.**

Step 3: Release the Energy with Intention

Place your hand on your heart and take a deep breath. Visualize the block as a dark cloud in front of you. Now, imagine a golden light forming in your heart—this is your healing energy.

As you exhale, see the golden light expanding, dissolving the dark cloud. Silently or aloud, say:

"I release all karmic burdens that no longer serve me. I choose freedom. I choose healing. I choose peace."

Feel the shift as the heavy energy dissolves. You may experience warmth, tingling, or even tears—this is your body and soul letting go.

Step 4: Affirm the New Energy

Now, replace the old energy with a new intention. Say to yourself:

"I am free from past limitations. I am open to new possibilities. I am ready to receive the life I deserve."

Breathe deeply, feeling the truth of these words settling into your being.

Breaking the Cycle for Good

Clearing a karmic block is not just about releasing the past; it is about choosing different actions moving forward.

- If your block was around **self-worth,** start treating yourself with more compassion.

- If your block was around **relationships,** set new boundaries and attract healthier connections.

- If your block was around **success,** release fear and take bold steps toward your goals.

Karma is not about fate—it is about growth. Every time you choose a new, empowered response, you are rewriting your karmic story.

Right now, take a deep breath. You have already begun.

The 44 Karmic Lessons—What Your Soul is Trying to Learn

Every soul comes into this life carrying lessons it needs to learn. Some are about love, others about patience, forgiveness, or self-worth. These lessons shape our experiences, guiding us toward spiritual growth and self-realization.

If you have ever felt like you are repeating the same patterns over and over—whether in relationships, finances, or self-confidence—it may not be bad luck. It is **a karmic lesson that has yet to be learned.**

Understanding your karmic lessons helps you break free from cycles that no longer serve you, allowing you to move forward with clarity, wisdom, and inner peace.

How Karmic Lessons Show Up in Your Life

Karmic lessons often appear through challenges. The same kinds of people, situations, or emotional struggles may keep resurfacing until you recognize what your soul is being asked to learn.

Have you ever:

- Attracted the same type of unhealthy relationships despite wanting something different?

- Struggled with confidence or self-worth no matter how much you achieve?

- Found yourself repeating financial struggles, even when opportunities are present?

These are signs that **a lesson is waiting to be acknowledged.** Once you consciously recognize it, the cycle can be broken.

The 44 Karmic Lessons & Their Meaning

Below are some of the most common karmic lessons souls come to master. As you read through them, notice if any deeply resonate with you. That is a sign that your soul is working through that lesson.

Lessons in Self-Worth & Confidence

1. Learning to love and accept yourself as you are.
2. Releasing the need for external validation.
3. Standing up for yourself and setting strong boundaries.
4. Knowing that you deserve happiness and success.
5. Letting go of comparison and embracing your own path.

Lessons in Love & Relationships

6. Understanding that love should never require self-sacrifice.
7. Recognizing when a relationship is teaching you growth versus when it is causing harm.
8. Releasing toxic attachments and learning to walk away with love.
9. Allowing yourself to receive love without fear.
10. Trusting that the right people will stay in your life without force or control.

Lessons in Forgiveness & Letting Go

11. Releasing resentment and understanding that forgiveness is for your peace.

12. Letting go of past mistakes and practicing self-compassion.

13. Learning to detach from painful experiences without carrying them forward.

14. Accepting that closure does not always come from others—it comes from within.

15. Trusting that everything that happens serves a higher purpose.

Lessons in Trust & Surrender

16. Learning to trust the timing of your life.

17. Letting go of the need to control everything.

18. Understanding that uncertainty is part of growth.

19. Recognizing that obstacles are often redirections toward something better.

20. Releasing fear and trusting that life is working in your favor.

Lessons in Boundaries & Personal Power

21. Knowing when to say no without guilt.

22. Protecting your energy from people who drain you.

23. Understanding that your worth is not measured by how much you give to others.

24. Stepping into your personal power without fear of judgment.

25. Breaking free from people-pleasing and choosing authenticity.

Lessons in Abundance & Success

26. Overcoming the belief that success is only for certain people.

27. Understanding that abundance is an energy, not just a financial state.

28. Releasing fears of failure and knowing that every setback is a step forward.

29. Trusting your ability to create the life you desire.

30. Letting go of limiting beliefs around money and success.

Lessons in Inner Peace & Emotional Balance

31. Learning that happiness is an internal state, not dependent on external circumstances.

32. Releasing attachment to past pain and choosing peace instead.

33. Recognizing that emotions are temporary and do not define you.

34. Practicing mindfulness and being present in the moment.

35. Choosing joy even in the midst of challenges.

Lessons in Purpose & Spiritual Growth

36. Trusting your inner wisdom instead of seeking answers outside of yourself.

37. Understanding that your challenges are part of your spiritual evolution.

38. Discovering your life purpose and following your soul's calling.

39. Releasing fears around stepping into your true power.

40. Knowing that your journey is unfolding exactly as it should.

Lessons in Unconditional Love & Unity

41. Seeing the divine in yourself and others.

42. Letting go of judgment and embracing compassion.

43. Recognizing that we are all connected, and what you give out, you receive.

44. Learning that love is not about possession, but about freedom and trust.

How to Identify & Heal Your Karmic Lessons

Now that you have read through the karmic lessons, take a moment to reflect.

- Which ones resonated with you the most?

- Which ones feel like ongoing struggles in your life?

- Are there patterns that you are now seeing more clearly?

Awareness is the first step toward breaking karmic cycles. Once you see the lesson, you can begin making different choices—choosing love over fear, trust over doubt, and growth over stagnation.

Take a deep breath and recognize how far you have already come. Every challenge you have faced has been guiding you toward wisdom, strength, and healing.

You are not stuck. You are evolving.

Daily Energy Detox—A Powerful Routine for Emotional Balance

Just as you cleanse your body every day, your energy field also requires regular purification. Throughout the day, you absorb energies from people, places, and experiences. Some of these are uplifting, but others can weigh you down, creating emotional exhaustion, stress, or even unexplained heaviness.

Energy detoxing is not just about removing negativity—it is about resetting, rebalancing, and protecting your energy so that you feel lighter, clearer, and emotionally strong. By integrating simple cleansing practices into your daily routine, you can maintain emotional balance, prevent energetic overload, and strengthen your inner peace.

Let us create a powerful energy detox routine that you can practice every day to clear unwanted energy and restore harmony.

Step 1: The Morning Reset—Start Your Day Clean & Protected

The way you begin your day sets the tone for everything that follows. Instead of rushing into your phone, emails, or social media, take the first few moments of your day to cleanse your energy and set a powerful intention.

Morning Energy Detox Practice:

- **Before getting out of bed, place your hand on your heart.** Take three deep breaths, feeling the rise and fall of your chest.

- **Visualize a golden light surrounding you,** dissolving any tension or lingering emotions from yesterday.

- **Silently affirm:** "Today, I choose peace. I protect my energy. Only positivity flows to me and through me."

This simple practice helps you wake up with **clarity, presence, and emotional strength.**

Step 2: Midday Check-In—Releasing Accumulated Energy

As you go through the day, your energy field interacts with countless people and situations. Sometimes, you unknowingly take on stress, frustration, or emotional heaviness from others. A quick midday reset ensures that you do not carry unwanted energy forward.

Midday Energy Detox Practice:

- Find a quiet space (even if it is just for a few minutes).

- Take a deep breath and shake your hands out, as if releasing any stagnant energy.

- Close your eyes and visualize a soft breeze passing through your body, **clearing away any heaviness or tension.**

- Say silently or aloud: *"I release all energy that does not belong to me. I reclaim my peace."*

This allows you to **reset your emotional state and continue your day with renewed energy.**

Step 3: Evening Cleansing—Releasing the Day's Energy

By the end of the day, your body and mind have absorbed many experiences. Carrying these energies into sleep can lead to restlessness, overthinking, or emotional drainage. An evening energy cleanse ensures that you release the day's weight and restore balance before resting.

Evening Energy Detox Practice:

- **Take a warm shower or a salt bath.** As the water flows over you, imagine it washing away any negativity, stress, or emotional residue.

- **Do a simple body scan.** Close your eyes and notice any tension in your body. Breathe into those areas, allowing them to soften and relax.

- **Visualize a cocoon of protective light around you.** Feel yourself surrounded by warmth, safety, and peace.

- **Before sleeping, affirm:** *"I release this day. I let go of all that no longer serves me. My body, mind, and soul are now at peace."*

This nightly detox helps your subconscious mind clear, heal, and recharge as you sleep.

Additional Energy Detox Practices for Extra Support

Some days feel heavier than others. When you sense a deep need for cleansing, here are additional practices you can incorporate:

- Burning sage or palo santo to clear stagnant energy from your home and aura.

- Walking barefoot on grass to ground yourself and reconnect with natural energy.

- Listening to high-frequency sounds like Tibetan singing bowls or ocean waves to balance your energy field.

- Writing down your worries and tearing up the paper to symbolically release mental burdens.

By making energy detoxing a daily habit, you will notice a profound shift—feeling **lighter, stronger, and more emotionally balanced** no matter what life brings.

Take a deep breath. You are releasing. You are cleansing. You are stepping into clarity.

LIFESTYLE & ENVIRONMENTAL HEALING: DETOX YOUR SPACE, DETOX YOUR SOUL

Protect Your Energy—How to Cut Off Negative People

Not everyone deserves access to your energy. Some people uplift you, inspire you, and bring peace into your life. Others drain you, manipulate you, or leave you feeling exhausted.

Energy is exchanged in every interaction. When you spend time with someone, you are not just sharing words—you are sharing vibrations. If you constantly feel depleted around certain people, it is a sign that their energy is not aligned with yours.

Learning to **protect your energy** is not selfish; it is necessary for your well-being. Setting boundaries and cutting off toxic influences allows you to create space for peace, clarity, and personal growth.

Recognizing Energy Drainers in Your Life

Some negative people are obvious—the ones who are always complaining, criticizing, or bringing conflict. But others may be more subtle. They can be people who seem kind but constantly guilt-trip you, demand your time, or make you feel small in their presence.

Signs that someone is draining your energy:

- You feel emotionally exhausted after interacting with them.

- You start doubting yourself or feeling anxious in their presence.

- They are always taking but rarely giving.

- You feel like you have to "walk on eggshells" around them.

- They dismiss your feelings, dreams, or personal boundaries.

If any of these signs resonate with you, it may be time to **distance yourself and reclaim your energy.**

How to Cut Off Negative People Without Guilt

Many people hesitate to walk away from toxic relationships because they feel guilty. But here is an important truth: **Your peace matters more than their expectations.**

Step 1: Stop Engaging in Their Drama

Negative people thrive on reactions. If they can trigger you, they feel powerful. The moment you stop feeding their negativity—by refusing to argue, over-explain, or seek their approval—you break their control over your energy.

Step 2: Set Boundaries with Confidence

Boundaries are not about controlling others; they are about **protecting yourself.** If someone constantly drains you, be clear about what you will and will not tolerate.

Instead of over-explaining, keep it simple:

- "I am focusing on my well-being, and I need space."
- "I am not available for this conversation."
- "I will no longer tolerate disrespect in my life."

Boundaries do not require permission. They require self-respect.

Step 3: Limit Access to Your Energy

If cutting someone off completely is not possible—such as a coworker or family member—create emotional distance. Keep interactions brief, avoid deep conversations, and do not let their energy influence your mood.

One powerful practice is **the "gray rock method"**—responding with neutral, minimal engagement. When you do not react, their ability to drain you diminishes.

Step 4: Protect Your Energy Spiritually

Energetic protection is just as important as physical protection. Before interacting with draining people, visualize yourself surrounded by a shield of light. This invisible boundary prevents negativity from entering your space.

You can also:

- Carry a black tourmaline or obsidian crystal for energy protection.

- Say a silent affirmation: "I am protected. No negative energy can affect me."

- Take a deep breath and mentally "wash away" any negativity after leaving their presence.

Step 5: Release the Emotional Ties

Sometimes, even after walking away, we feel emotionally tied to negative people. This is because **unspoken energy still lingers.**

To fully release them, try this:

- Write a letter expressing everything you feel—then burn or tear it up.

- Practice the **cord-cutting visualization** to dissolve emotional attachments.

- **Affirm:** *"I release you with love, and I reclaim my energy."*

The more you focus on **your own healing,** the less power their presence will have over you.

Your Energy is Sacred—Protect It Fiercely

Not everyone is meant to walk with you on your journey. Some people are lessons, some are distractions, and some are detours. But you always have the power to choose who stays and who does not.

Choosing peace over toxicity is not cruelty—it is self-care.

Take a deep breath. Feel your energy returning to you. You are no longer available for anything that drains your soul.

Declutter Your Home & Mind—Why Cleaning Up Changes Everything

Your outer world is a reflection of your inner world. If your home, workspace, or surroundings feel cluttered and chaotic, chances are your mind is carrying the same weight.

Many people underestimate the power of decluttering, thinking it is only about physical tidiness. But in reality, **removing physical clutter clears mental and emotional blockages, creating space for new energy, ideas, and clarity.**

If you have been feeling stuck, uninspired, or emotionally drained, it may not be your thoughts that need shifting—it may be your environment.

How Clutter Affects Your Mind & Energy

Every object in your space carries energy. When your environment is messy, overfilled, or disorganized, it sends subtle signals to your mind, leading to stress, distraction, and even emotional heaviness.

Studies show that clutter increases cortisol levels (the stress hormone), making it harder to focus, relax, or feel at peace. It also keeps you mentally stuck in the past, surrounded by unfinished projects, outdated memories, and things you no longer need.

Decluttering is not just about letting go of objects—it is about making room for a fresh start.

The Deep Decluttering Method: Clearing Space for New Energy

If you want to shift your mindset, clear stagnant energy, and create space for abundance, follow this **four-step decluttering process.**

Step 1: Choose One Area to Start With

Trying to declutter everything at once can feel overwhelming. Instead, start small. Choose one space—a drawer, a closet, your workspace.

As you go through your items, ask yourself:

- **Does this bring me peace or stress?**
- **Do I truly need this, or am I keeping it out of guilt or habit?**
- **Does this object reflect the life I want to create?**

If something no longer aligns with you, **let it go.**

Step 2: The "Letting Go" Practice

Many people hold onto clutter because of emotional attachment. The best way to release items is to express gratitude for them.

Before donating or discarding something, hold it in your hands and say:

"Thank you for serving me. I release you with love."

This practice allows you to let go without guilt, making space for **new energy to flow.**

Step 3: Organize with Intention

Once you have removed what no longer serves you, arrange your space in a way that brings **calmness and clarity.**

- Keep items that inspire joy and motivation.
- Use natural elements (plants, crystals, candles) to uplift the energy.
- Ensure that each item has a purpose—if it does not, reconsider its place in your space.

Your environment should feel like a **sacred, supportive space** that nourishes your soul.

Step 4: Maintain a Daily Energy Reset

Decluttering is not just a one-time task—it is a habit of **energy maintenance.**

Every evening, take a few minutes to:

- Clear unnecessary items from your workspace.

- Open windows to let fresh air in.

- Burn incense, light a candle, or play calming music to refresh the energy.

These small actions help you **end the day with clarity and wake up with a fresh mindset.**

Decluttering Your Digital & Mental Space

Clutter is not just physical—it exists in the digital and mental realms as well.

- **Digital Clutter:** Unsubscribe from emails that overwhelm you, delete unused apps, and clear old files that no longer serve you.

- **Mental Clutter:** If your mind feels overloaded, try journaling to release scattered thoughts, practicing mindfulness, or scheduling "quiet time" away from distractions.

Every time you remove what is no longer needed, you **create space for clarity, inspiration, and new opportunities.**

Decluttering is an Act of Self-Respect

When you clear your space, you are not just tidying up—you are **aligning your energy with peace, focus, and abundance.**

Right now, look around. What is one thing you can release today to make room for something better?

Take a deep breath. Let go of what is weighing you down.

You are creating space for something new.

Sacred Spaces—How to Create a Healing Corner at Home

Your home is more than just a physical space—it is an extension of your energy. The way you arrange and care for your environment directly influences your emotional state, your thoughts, and even your ability to heal.

When life feels overwhelming, having a **dedicated healing space** can serve as a sanctuary, a place where you can reconnect with yourself, recharge, and find clarity. This is not about creating a lavish meditation room or following complex rituals. It is about **intentionally designing a small, peaceful corner that nurtures your soul.**

Even in the busiest homes, a sacred space can bring grounding, balance, and emotional healing.

Why You Need a Sacred Space

In today's world, our energy is constantly scattered—between work, social obligations, and digital distractions. Having a **designated healing space** helps you:

- Create a daily practice of self-care and reflection.
- Reduce stress and reset your energy after a long day.
- Strengthen your connection to your inner self.
- Invite peace and clarity into your life.

A sacred space is not just about where you sit—it is about **what you experience within it.**

How to Create Your Own Healing Corner

You do not need a large room or expensive décor. Even a small section of your bedroom, living room, or balcony can become a powerful place for healing.

Step 1: Choose a Space That Feels Right

Look around your home and find a spot that naturally feels calm. It could be a quiet corner, a window seat, or a space near a plant.

If possible, choose an area with natural light, as sunlight carries **cleansing and uplifting energy.**

Step 2: Clear the Energy First

Before setting up your sacred space, remove any clutter or distractions. A clean space allows for **clear energy flow.**

To cleanse the area:

- Burn sage, palo santo, or incense to clear stagnant energy.

- Sprinkle salt in the corners and let it sit for a few hours before sweeping it away.

- Open windows and let fresh air circulate, inviting new energy into the space.

Once the energy is clear, you are ready to create a **healing atmosphere.**

Step 3: Add Elements That Bring You Peace

Your sacred space should **reflect what soothes and uplifts you. Consider adding:**

- **Crystals** – Amethyst for peace, rose quartz for love, or black tourmaline for protection.

- **Candles or Essential Oils** – Lavender, sandalwood, or frankincense help create a calm environment.

- **A Comfortable Cushion or Chair** – A place where you can sit and breathe without discomfort.

- **Sacred Symbols** – A small statue, spiritual artwork, or any object that carries personal meaning.

- **Nature Elements** – Plants, flowers, or a small bowl of water to bring balance and harmony.

Each item in your space should **carry intention and purpose.** Choose things that make you feel safe, inspired, and connected.

Using Your Sacred Space for Healing

Now that your healing corner is set up, how do you use it?

This space is for **any practice that nourishes your soul.** You might:

- Meditate or practice breathwork.

- Journal your thoughts and emotions.

- Read inspiring books or spiritual texts.

- Sit in silence and reconnect with your inner self.

- Practice gratitude by reflecting on the blessings in your life.

It is not about spending hours there—it is about consistency. Even 5-10 minutes in your sacred space each day can reset your energy and bring you back to balance.

Maintaining the Energy of Your Sacred Space

Energy in your home shifts based on what happens around it. To keep your healing corner vibrant:

- **Cleanse it regularly** by smudging, playing soft music, or simply expressing gratitude for the space.

- **Refresh the space** by changing elements occasionally—adding fresh flowers, updating affirmations, or rotating crystals.

- **Use it with intention**—whenever you feel overwhelmed, step into this space as a reminder that peace is always available to you.

Your sacred space is **not just a physical corner—it is a portal to stillness, clarity, and healing.**

Take a deep breath. This space belongs to you.

Morning Healing Rituals—Start Your Day with Strength & Peace

The first few moments after waking up set the tone for your entire day. If you begin the morning feeling rushed, overwhelmed, or consumed by stress, that energy carries into everything you do. But when you start your day with **intention, balance, and self-care,** you cultivate inner peace and mental clarity that stay with you throughout the day.

Healing is not just something that happens during deep meditation or therapy sessions—it is in the small, daily rituals that reconnect you to yourself. A simple morning healing practice can shift your energy, clear negativity, and strengthen your emotional well-being.

The Power of a Healing Morning Routine

Your mind is in its most receptive state when you wake up. This is the perfect time to cleanse, align, and set intentions. Morning healing rituals help you:

- Clear emotional residue from the previous day.
- Strengthen your mindset before external influences take over.
- Protect your energy from stress and negativity.
- Increase focus, creativity, and emotional resilience.

You do not need to spend hours on a morning routine. Even **5–10 minutes** of conscious healing practice can create a powerful shift.

The Healing Morning Ritual: A Step-by-Step Guide

Step 1: Wake Up with Awareness

The moment you wake up, resist the urge to check your phone, emails, or messages. Instead, take a deep breath and place your hand on your heart. Feel the warmth of your own presence.

Before even getting out of bed, silently affirm:

"I am awake. I am alive. I am grateful for this day."

This small act **grounds you in gratitude and resets your energy.**

Step 2: Cleanse Your Energy with Water

Water is a natural energy purifier. As you wash your face or take a morning shower, visualize the water **washing away any negativity or emotional heaviness.**

As the water flows over you, affirm:

"I release all that no longer serves me. I welcome clarity, peace, and renewal."

If possible, add a pinch of **Himalayan salt** to your morning shower for extra energetic cleansing.

Step 3: Breathwork for Energy & Balance

Your breath is the fastest way to shift your energy. A simple **3-minute breathwork practice** helps activate clarity and focus.

Try this:

- Inhale deeply for **4 seconds,** feeling the breath expand your chest.
- Hold for **4 seconds,** letting the energy settle.
- Exhale slowly for **6 seconds,** releasing tension.
- Repeat this cycle **five times.**

As you breathe, imagine fresh, pure energy filling your

body, replacing any fatigue or stress.

Step 4: Morning Affirmations to Rewire Your Mind

What you tell yourself in the morning shapes your subconscious mind. Instead of letting old doubts and worries take over, consciously set empowering thoughts for the day.

Stand in front of a mirror and say:

"I am strong, calm, and capable."

"I attract peace, joy, and abundance."

"No matter what happens today, I remain centered and grounded."

Saying affirmations aloud, while looking into your own eyes, **reinforces them deep into your subconscious.**

Step 5: Protect Your Energy Before Stepping Out

Before leaving your home or starting work, take a moment to **shield your energy.**

Close your eyes and visualize **a protective sphere of golden light** surrounding you. This light acts as a barrier, allowing only positive, supportive energy into your space.

Silently affirm:

"I am protected. I am surrounded by peace. I carry my own calmness wherever I go."

This practice prevents external negativity from affecting you, allowing you to move through the day with greater ease and focus.

Creating a Morning Routine That Works for You

The key to a healing morning ritual is **consistency.** Start with just one or two practices that resonate with you, and gradually build from there.

Even if you only have a few minutes, prioritize the practices that make you feel centered, strong, and clear-headed.

Your morning is your foundation—**build it with care.**

Take a deep breath. You are ready for the day.

The Healing Power of Silence—How Quiet Time Clears the Mind

In a world filled with constant noise—notifications, conversations, endless distractions—silence has become rare. Yet, silence is where healing begins.

Most people fear silence because it forces them to confront their own thoughts. But what if silence is not empty? What if it is **a doorway to clarity, inner peace, and emotional healing?**

The practice of embracing silence is not just about turning off external noise—it is about **creating a space where your mind and emotions can breathe, reset, and find balance.**

If you feel overwhelmed, restless, or disconnected from yourself, this chapter will guide you through the **powerful practice of silence as a tool for deep transformation.**

Why Silence is a Healing Force

Every time you sit in silence, you give your nervous system a chance to reset. Studies show that even **two minutes of complete silence** can lower stress hormones, reduce anxiety, and improve focus.

Silence also strengthens your intuition. When you remove external distractions, you begin to hear the wisdom that has always been within you.

Many spiritual masters, from monks to healers, have used silence as a way to **clear mental clutter, detach from negativity, and reconnect with their higher self.**

But you do not have to be a monk to experience the benefits. You simply need to **allow silence into your daily** life.

The Deep Silence Healing Practice

This simple practice will help you use silence as a tool for emotional clarity and energetic cleansing.

Step 1: Find a Space Without Distractions

Choose a quiet spot where you will not be disturbed. Turn off your phone, close the door, and remove any background noise.

Step 2: Sit with Yourself—No Music, No Guided Meditation

Most people use background noise to avoid their thoughts. But true healing happens when you sit in pure silence and let whatever needs to arise, arise.

At first, this might feel uncomfortable. Your mind will race. You may feel restless. That is normal. **Do not resist it—simply observe.**

Step 3: Observe Your Inner Dialogue

Instead of pushing thoughts away, notice them like clouds passing in the sky. Ask yourself:

- What emotions come up when I sit in silence?
- What is my mind constantly repeating?
- Are these thoughts serving me, or are they old patterns?

Silence reveals what is hidden beneath the surface. The more you practice, the more clarity you will gain.

Step 4: Let Go of Mental Noise

If your mind keeps racing, do not force it to stop. Instead, focus on **your breath.** With each inhale, imagine fresh, peaceful energy entering your body. With each exhale, visualize stress, worries, and mental noise dissolving.

As you continue, you will notice a shift—the noise inside you will start to fade, replaced by a deep stillness.

Step 5: Ask Yourself One Powerful Question

When your mind becomes quieter, ask yourself:

"What is my soul trying to tell me?"

Let the answer arise naturally. It may come as a thought, a feeling, or just a deep sense of knowing. This is the power of silence—**it allows your inner wisdom to speak.**

Integrating Silence into Your Daily Life

You do not need hours of silence to experience its benefits. Just **five to ten minutes of stillness each day** can bring profound clarity.

* Begin your mornings with a few minutes of silent reflection.

* Turn off music or podcasts during walks and listen to nature.

* Take silent breaks throughout your day to reset your mind.

* End your evenings with quiet time instead of screen time.

The more you embrace silence, the more **you will hear yourself.** And when you hear yourself clearly, healing becomes effortless.

Right now, close your eyes. Take a deep breath. Feel the peace within the silence.

You are not lost. You are simply rediscovering yourself.

Becoming the Best Version of Yourself—A Roadmap to Inner Peace

Healing is not just about overcoming pain—it is about transforming into the best version of yourself. It is about stepping into a life where you no longer react from wounds, but from wisdom. Where you are no longer held back by fear, but guided by inner peace.

But self-transformation does not happen overnight. It is a **process of unlearning old patterns, making new choices, and showing up for yourself every single day.**

This chapter is not about becoming "perfect." It is about becoming **real—aligned with your highest self, free from emotional baggage, and fully present in your own life.**

Let us begin.

Step 1: Identify the Old Version of You That No Longer Serves You

Before you can transform, you need to recognize what needs to change. Look at your current habits, thoughts, and behaviors. Which ones are holding you back?

Ask yourself:

- Do I often doubt myself or put myself down?
- Do I let fear dictate my decisions?
- Do I hold onto relationships, habits, or beliefs that no longer serve me?

The **best version of you** is already inside—it is just buried under layers of conditioning, past pain, and limiting beliefs. The first step to transformation is **recognizing what needs to go.**

Step 2: Create a New Identity for Yourself

Your current reality is a result of your past thoughts and choices. If you want a different future, you must start by **seeing yourself differently.**

Close your eyes and visualize your highest self—the person you truly want to become.

- How does this version of you think, feel, and act?
- How does this version of you handle challenges?

- What habits, routines, and beliefs shape this person's life?

Write down a **new self-identity statement:**

"I am someone who prioritizes my peace. I trust myself completely. I no longer seek validation—I create my own happiness. I release the past, step into my power, and allow myself to grow."

The more you repeat this, the more your subconscious mind will accept it as your new reality.

Step 3: Build Daily Habits That Support Your Transformation

Self-transformation is not about one big change—it is about **small, consistent actions that create lasting shifts.**

Choose one or two habits that align with your best self and commit to them daily.

- If your best self is confident, start practicing **positive self-talk.**

- If your best self is emotionally strong, start practicing **mindfulness and emotional awareness.**

- If your best self is healthy, start making **nourishing food and movement choices.**

It does not have to be perfect. Progress matters more than speed.

Step 4: Heal the Wounds That Hold You Back

Often, what stops people from becoming their best selves is **unresolved emotional pain.** Old traumas, heartbreaks, or self-doubt can create unconscious resistance to growth.

To truly step into your highest potential, you must **heal, not suppress.**

Try this healing exercise:

1. Write down one emotional wound that still affects you.

2. Ask yourself: What belief did this experience create in me?

3. Rewrite the belief into a positive affirmation.

For example:

- If past rejection made you feel unworthy, affirm: *"I am deeply worthy of love and belonging."*

- If childhood criticism made you fear failure, affirm: *"I allow myself to grow without judgment."*

The more you heal, the more **you free yourself to become the person you were always meant to be.**

Step 5: Surround Yourself with Growth Energy

The people, content, and environments you expose yourself to shape your mindset. If you are constantly around negativity, doubt, or stagnation, it will slow your growth.

Choose to **surround yourself with people and influences that elevate you.**

- Spend time with those who inspire and support your transformation.

- Consume books, podcasts, and teachings that expand your thinking.

- Remove yourself from toxic environments that keep you stuck.

The best version of you **thrives in a space that nurtures growth.**

Step 6: Trust the Process—Transformation is a Journey

Becoming your best self is not a one-time event—it is a lifelong journey. Some days will feel easy, and others will feel like setbacks. But as long as you keep moving forward, you are growing.

Whenever you feel lost, return to these three truths:

- You are not your past. Every moment is a chance to start fresh.
- Growth is uncomfortable, but staying stuck is worse.
- You do not have to be perfect—just committed to your evolution.

The best version of you **is already within you.** Your only job is to let go of what is not you and step fully into your truth.

Right now, take a deep breath. You are already transforming.

Stop Touching the Wound—How to Let Go of Pain for Good

Healing is not about constantly revisiting the past. It is about releasing it. Yet, many people unknowingly keep their wounds open by replaying old memories, revisiting painful conversations, and holding onto resentment.

If you had a physical wound, you would not keep touching it every day, expecting it to heal. The same applies to emotional wounds. The more you revisit the pain, the more it lingers. True healing happens when you **stop feeding the wound and start allowing yourself to move forward.**

This chapter is about **breaking the cycle of emotional pain** so you can finally let go and reclaim your peace.

Why We Keep Touching the Wound

Many people hold onto pain because it has become familiar. Even though it hurts, it feels like a part of them. Some replay painful memories to find closure. Others cling to resentment as a form of protection, fearing that letting go means the pain was meaningless.

But holding onto pain does not change the past—it only keeps you trapped in it.

Pain is meant to be processed, not carried forever. **The moment you decide to stop engaging with it, healing begins.**

The Letting Go Process: A Transformational Healing Exercise

If you have been holding onto past pain, this exercise will help you **release it fully and move forward.**

Step 1: Identify the Wound You Keep Reopening

Close your eyes and ask yourself: What past event or memory do I keep revisiting?

It might be a betrayal, a heartbreak, a failure, or a moment that deeply hurt you. Write it down without filtering your emotions.

Step 2: Ask Yourself—What Am I Gaining by Holding Onto This?

Pain, as much as it hurts, often serves a hidden purpose. It might:

- Keep you feeling connected to someone who hurt you.

- Validate your anger, making you feel "right" about what happened.

- Give you an excuse to stay stuck instead of moving forward.

Be honest with yourself. What is this pain giving you? And is it truly worth it?

Step 3: Reframe the Pain—Turn It into a Lesson

Instead of seeing this wound as something that broke you, **see it as something that taught you.**

Ask yourself: *What did this experience teach me? What strength did I gain from it?*

For example:

- If someone betrayed you, it may have taught you to trust yourself more.

- If you experienced rejection, it may have guided you toward something better.

- If you went through loss, it may have deepened your understanding of love.

Once you see the **lesson in the pain,** it loses its power over you.

Step 4: Release the Emotional Weight

Take a deep breath and visualize yourself holding this wound in your hands. Now, imagine placing it inside a box and sealing it shut.

Silently affirm:

"I am done carrying this pain. I will release it now. I set myself free."

Then, visualize the box dissolving into light. Feel the weight lifting off you.

You are no longer trapped by this memory. You are free.

Healing Means Moving Forward

Letting go doesn't mean forgetting. It does not mean what happened was okay. It simply means **you are choosing your peace over your pain.**

You cannot rewrite the past, but you can **choose what you focus on moving forward.** Every time you stop yourself from revisiting the wound, you take another step toward full healing.

Right now, take a deep breath. Feel the relief of **no longer carrying what was never meant to define you.**

You are stepping into a new chapter—one that is free, light, and full of possibility.

ALTERNATIVE HEALING & TRANSFORMATIONAL TECHNIQUES: UNLOCK HIDDEN HEALING POWERS

Full Moon Rituals—How to Release What No Longer Serves You

The full moon has long been regarded as a **celestial crucible**—a moment when energy reaches its peak, emotions rise to the surface, and the universe beckons us to **release, renew, and transcend.** Just as the moon orchestrates the tides, it also stirs the depths of our inner world, urging us to let go of what no longer serves us.

Ancient traditions across cultures have revered the full moon as a time of **purging, healing, and reimagining** one's path. Its luminous glow illuminates what is hidden in the shadows of our psyche, guiding us through the labyrinth of self-discovery.

If you find yourself weighed down by old wounds, fears, or limiting beliefs, this ritual will help you cleanse your spirit, making space for **verdant growth, fresh beginnings, and renewed clarity.**

Why Full Moon Rituals Are So Powerful

Every phase of the moon holds a unique energy, but the **full moon is a peak moment of illumination and release.** It is when the intricate tapestry of our emotions, thoughts, and experiences intertwine, forming a mirror that reflects what we need to shed.

During this time, unresolved emotions rise to the surface. The **enlightening yet enigmatic** glow of the moon urges you to acknowledge and release what no longer aligns with your highest self. Whether it be toxic relationships, self-doubt, old narratives, or fears that keep you confined in a mental labyrinth, the full moon **beckons you to let go and realign.**

The Full Moon Release Ritual

This transformative practice will help you **embark on a journey of surrender, renewal, and deep healing.**

Step 1: Create a Sacred Space

Find a quiet place where you can immerse yourself in this ritual. Nature is ideal—a garden, a balcony under the stars, or even a peaceful indoor space with an open window. Arrange a few **mystical victuals**—a cup of herbal tea, fruits, or nuts—to nourish both body and spirit as you delve into the practice.

Light a candle or incense, allowing its fragrance to intertwine with the air, signaling to your subconscious that you are entering a sacred space.

Step 2: Write Down What You Wish to Release

Take a journal or a simple piece of paper and write down **everything that is weighing on your soul.** This could be:

- A habit that no longer serves you.
- A fear that keeps you small.
- Emotional wounds you are ready to heal.
- A relationship that has run its course.

Do not hold back. Let the emotions flow onto the page like an intricate mosaic of past experiences that you are now ready to dissolve.

Step 3: The Fire & Water Release

Once you have poured your emotions onto paper, choose one of two ways to **orchestrate the act of release:**

- **Fire Release:** Safely burn the paper in a bowl or fireplace, watching the flames **transcend your burdens into light and smoke.** As the fire consumes the words, silently affirm:

  "I release this with love. It no longer defines me."

- Water Release: Tear the paper into small pieces and immerse them in a bowl of water, visualizing the words dissolving. Water, symbolic of flow and renewal, **carries away stagnant energy** and makes space for transformation.

Step 4: Absorb the Full Moon's Cleansing Energy

Stand beneath the moon, feeling its gentle yet powerful energy envelop you like a celestial embrace. Close your eyes and **breathe deeply, envisioning a silvery light washing over you, purging all that no longer belongs in your spirit.**

Place your hands over your heart and affirm:

"I am light. I am free. I am stepping into a reimagined version of myself."

Let the moon be your witness as you **orchestrate this moment of liberation.**

Integrating the Full Moon's Magic into Your Life

The work does not end with the ritual. Carry the essence of this release forward by:

- Keeping your energy clear with meditation or grounding practices.
- Avoiding situations that rekindle the emotions you just released.
- Journaling about how you feel in the days following the ritual.
- Creating new affirmations that align with your **reimagined self.**

Each full moon invites you to step deeper into your evolution, shedding what is outdated and **embarking on a more aligned, authentic journey.**

Take a deep breath. The past no longer holds you. You are lighter, freer, and open to the **kaleidoscopic possibilities** that lie ahead.

Healing Through Travel—Why a Change of Place Can Change Your Life

Sometimes, healing does not come from thinking, talking, or analyzing—it comes from movement. There is something powerful about stepping out of your everyday surroundings, leaving behind familiar patterns, and placing yourself in a new environment. **Travel is not just about seeing new places; it is about rediscovering yourself in ways you never expected.**

Many ancient cultures understood this deeply. Pilgrimages, sacred journeys, and time spent in nature have long been used as tools for healing and transformation. Whether you travel to a distant land, a quiet retreat, or simply take a break from your daily routine, the experience **shifts your energy, clears emotional stagnation, and awakens new perspectives.**

If you have been feeling stuck, uninspired, or weighed down by life, this chapter will show you how **travel can be a powerful catalyst for healing.**

Why Travel Heals the Soul

Your mind and body thrive on new experiences. When you immerse yourself in a different environment, your senses awaken, your perspectives expand, and your spirit feels recharged. Travel breaks patterns. It forces you to be present. It allows you to see yourself outside of your normal identity.

How travel creates deep healing:

- **Detachment from past energy:** When you leave behind your usual surroundings, you naturally create emotional distance from old memories, stress, and repetitive thoughts.

- **Exposure to new perspectives:** Seeing different ways of life broadens your understanding of yourself and the world.

- **Connection with nature:** Traveling to mountains, forests, oceans, or sacred places rejuvenates your energy field and resets your emotional balance.

- **Space for self-reflection:** Being in an unfamiliar place removes distractions, making it easier to reconnect with your inner self.

The real healing happens **not just in the journey itself, but in the way it changes you.**

The Healing Travel Experience: A Guide to Transformational Journeys

You do not need to fly to a distant country to experience the healing power of travel. Even a simple weekend getaway, a solo retreat, or a walk in a different part of your city can create a shift.

Here are ways to turn **any travel experience into a healing journey:**

1. Travel with Intention

Instead of traveling just to escape, travel with a **purpose.** Before you leave, ask yourself:

- What do I need to release on this trip?

- What part of myself do I want to reconnect with?

- What do I want to invite into my life?

By setting an intention, your journey becomes more than just a change of scenery—it becomes a transformational experience.

2. Disconnect from Your Routine & External Noise

Healing travel requires presence. Reduce distractions by limiting phone usage, social media, or constant checking of work emails.

- If possible, keep a travel journal to document insights, emotions, and personal reflections.

- Avoid rushing from one place to another. Give yourself time to just **be.**

- Spend time alone in nature, absorbing the energy of your surroundings.

This space of stillness allows your **mind to settle, your heart to heal, and your spirit to awaken.**

3. Visit Places That Hold Healing Energy

Certain locations naturally hold a **higher vibrational energy** and have been known for centuries as places of healing. These include:

- **Mountains & Forests:** Grounding, calming, and spiritually uplifting.

- **Beaches & Oceans:** Cleansing, emotionally releasing, and deeply refreshing.

- **Temples & Sacred Sites:** High-energy places that help you reconnect with your soul.

- **Quiet Villages or Countryside:** A slower pace allows for deep self-reflection.

If you feel drawn to a certain place, **trust that your soul knows where it needs to go.**

4. Engage in a Self-Healing Travel Ritual

While traveling, take a moment each day for a simple ritual to ground your experience.

Morning Ritual: Before you start your day, take five deep breaths and affirm:

"I am open to whatever healing this journey brings."

Evening Reflection: At the end of the day, sit quietly and ask yourself:

- What did I learn about myself today?
- What emotions surfaced that need my attention?
- How do I feel different from when I arrived?

This conscious reflection makes travel more than just an experience—it turns it into **an internal transformation.**

Returning Home as a Changed Person

Travel is not just about what happens while you are away—it is about **how you integrate those lessons when you return.**

After coming back, notice what feels different:

- Do you see life from a new perspective?
- Do certain things that once stressed you now seem less important?
- Do you feel more at peace, confident, or open?

The best way to **keep the energy of healing travel alive** is to continue practicing presence, self-reflection, and openness to change—no matter where you are.

Healing is a Journey—Keep Walking

Sometimes, healing requires stepping away from what is familiar so you can see yourself more clearly. Travel is one of the most beautiful ways to break old cycles, invite new energy, and return to yourself in a deeper way.

If your soul has been longing for a shift, **maybe it is time to answer the call.**

Take a deep breath. The world is waiting for you, and so is your next transformation.

Oracle & Angel Cards—How to Use Them for Clarity & Guidance

There are moments in life when the mind feels clouded, decisions feel impossible, and you seek a sign—a whisper from the universe to guide you. This is where **oracle and angel cards** come in.

Unlike traditional tarot cards, which follow structured symbolism, oracle and angel cards are more fluid, intuitive, and deeply connected to your inner wisdom. They are not about predicting the future but about **bringing you clarity, insight, and confirmation of what your soul already knows.**

If you have ever felt drawn to these cards but were unsure how to use them, this chapter will guide you through the process of **using oracle and angel cards as a healing tool for self-reflection, guidance, and emotional balance.**

What Are Oracle & Angel Cards?

Oracle cards are decks with messages, symbols, or affirmations that help you gain insight into your current situation. Some focus on healing, some on spiritual guidance, and others on personal growth.

Angel cards, specifically, are designed to **connect you with the energy of angels, spirit guides, and higher wisdom.** They offer messages of love, reassurance, and support, especially in times of uncertainty.

The beauty of these cards is that **anyone can use them.** You do not need to be psychic or have any special abilities. You only need **openness, intention, and trust in your inner guidance.**

How Oracle & Angel Cards Help with Healing

Using oracle and angel cards is like having **a conversation with your higher self.** They reflect back to you the answers that already exist within you, helping you:

- Gain clarity when your mind feels overwhelmed.

- Receive confirmation about decisions or choices.

- Shift your perspective when you feel stuck.

- Feel spiritually supported during difficult times.

- Strengthen your intuition and inner wisdom.

They do not tell you what to do. Instead, they help you see things from a higher perspective so you can make empowered choices.

How to Use Oracle & Angel Cards for Self-Healing

If you are new to oracle or angel cards, follow this simple **step-by-step guide** to create a healing and intuitive reading for yourself.

Step 1: Set an Intention

Before you shuffle the deck, take a deep breath and set a clear intention. You might ask:

- What do I need to know right now?

- What energy should I focus on for healing?

- What guidance do my angels or higher self have for me?

Your intention is what directs the energy of the reading.

Step 2: Shuffle the Cards & Choose One (or More)

Hold the deck in your hands and shuffle gently. As you do, allow your intuition to guide you. You might:

- Feel drawn to a certain card.

- Notice a card "jumping" out of the deck.

- Select one randomly after shuffling.

There is no wrong way—**trust what feels natural.**

Step 3: Read the Message & Reflect

Turn over the card and read its message. If your deck comes with a guidebook, read the interpretation, but also pay attention to **what thoughts, emotions, or insights arise within you.**

Ask yourself:

- How does this message relate to what I am experiencing?
- What emotions does it bring up?
- What action or mindset shift does this card inspire?

Write down your reflections in a journal. Sometimes, the meaning of a card becomes clearer over time.

Step 4: Take Inspired Action

The purpose of using oracle or angel cards is not just to receive messages but to **apply them to your life.**

If a card encourages self-care, schedule time for it.

If it speaks of releasing the past, practice a letting-go ritual.

If it reassures you, allow yourself to **trust the journey.**

Your healing happens when you **align your actions with your guidance.**

Daily & Weekly Oracle Card Practices

To make oracle or angel cards a regular healing tool, try these simple practices:

- **Morning Guidance:** Pull a card each morning to set the tone for your day.
- **Full Moon & New Moon Rituals:** Use them during moon cycles to reflect and reset your energy.
- **Journaling Prompt:** Use the card's message as a theme for journaling and self-reflection.

- **Healing Support:** Whenever you feel lost or uncertain, draw a card to reconnect with your inner wisdom.

The more you work with your deck, the stronger your intuition will become.

Trusting Yourself Above All

Oracle and angel cards do not hold power over you. **You are the one with the power.** They are simply tools to awaken the guidance that already exists within you.

Your intuition is always speaking to you—through feelings, synchronicities, and inner nudges. These cards simply **help you listen more deeply.**

Take a deep breath. **You already know the answers you seek.**

EFT Tapping—A Simple Technique to Heal Emotional Pain

Emotions are energy. When they are processed in a healthy way, they flow freely. But when emotions are suppressed—due to stress, trauma, or fear—they get trapped in the body, creating emotional blocks, anxiety, and even physical pain.

Emotional Freedom Technique (EFT), also known as Tapping, is a simple yet powerful healing method that helps you release stuck emotions, reduce anxiety, and rewire negative thought patterns. It combines the principles of acupressure and psychology, using gentle tapping on specific energy points of the body to clear emotional and energetic blockages.

If you have been holding onto stress, fear, or self-doubt, this chapter will guide you through using EFT tapping as a transformative healing practice.

How EFT Tapping Works

EFT works by gently tapping on nine key meridian points of the body while focusing on a specific emotional issue. This sends a calming signal to the brain, reducing stress and shifting negative thought patterns.

Scientific research has shown that EFT lowers cortisol levels, the stress hormone, and can effectively help with anxiety, trauma, emotional pain, and even physical symptoms caused by emotional distress.

Think of it as acupuncture without needles—using your fingertips to restore balance to your body's energy system.

The Step-by-Step EFT Tapping Process

Follow this guided EFT tapping sequence to release emotional pain and restore inner peace.

Step 1: Identify the Emotion

Before tapping, become aware of what you are feeling. Ask yourself:

- What emotion am I struggling with? (Anxiety, sadness, guilt, anger, etc.)
- Where do I feel it in my body? (Tight chest, heavy heart, tension in shoulders, etc.)
- On a scale of 1 to 10, how intense is this emotion?

This awareness helps direct the healing process.

Step 2: Create a Setup Statement

The setup statement acknowledges what you are feeling while affirming self-acceptance.

It follows this formula:

"Even though I feel [emotion], I deeply and completely accept myself."

Example:

- *"Even though I feel anxious about the future, I deeply and completely accept myself."*
- *"Even though I feel unworthy of love, I choose to love and accept myself."*

Repeat this statement three times while tapping on the side of your hand (the karate chop point).

Step 3: Tap on the Meridian Points

Now, begin tapping on the following points, repeating a reminder phrase that reflects your emotion.

Use two fingers to gently tap 5–7 times on each point.

1. **Eyebrow Point (start of the eyebrow)** – "This anxiety…"
2. **Side of the Eye (temple area)** – "I feel so stuck…"
3. **Under the Eye (cheekbone)** – "I can't let this go…"
4. **Under the Nose (above the lip)** – "This emotion feels overwhelming…"
5. **Chin (below the lower lip)** – "What if I could release this?"
6. **Collarbone (base of the throat, slightly below the collarbone)** – "Maybe I don't have to hold onto this anymore…"
7. **Under the Arm (side of the ribcage, about four inches below the armpit)** – "I am ready to let this go…"
8. **Top of the Head (crown of the head)** – "I allow peace and healing to flow through me."

Take a deep breath and notice how your body feels.

Step 4: Reassess & Shift the Emotion

After one round of tapping, check in with yourself.

- Has the emotional intensity decreased?

- Do you feel any shifts in your body?

- What new thoughts or insights have surfaced?

Repeat the process, modifying your statements to reflect the change. For example:

"Even though I still feel some of this anxiety, I am choosing to let go of it now."

With each round, you may feel lighter, calmer, and more empowered.

When & How to Use EFT for Healing

EFT is a tool you can use anytime you feel overwhelmed, triggered, or emotionally stuck.

Use it for:

- **Daily stress relief** – A quick way to reset your nervous system.

- **Overcoming self-doubt** – Releasing limiting beliefs about yourself.

- **Emotional release** – Processing sadness, anger, guilt, or grief.

- **Anxiety & fears** – Calming your mind before a stressful situation.

With practice, EFT rewires your emotional responses, helping you replace old patterns with new, empowering beliefs.

Final Thought: Healing Through Self-Acceptance

The deepest healing happens when you allow yourself to feel, process, and release. EFT is a powerful yet simple way to remind your mind and body that you are safe, you are healing, and you are worthy of peace.

Take a deep breath. Tap gently on your heart. You are no longer holding onto pain—you are setting yourself free.

The Magic of Gratitude—How to Shift Your Energy Instantly

Gratitude is one of the most powerful healing forces in existence. It has the ability to rewire your brain, shift your energy, and instantly change the way you experience life.

When you focus on what is missing, you live in a state of lack. But when you focus on what you already have, you create a vibration of abundance. Gratitude is not about denying challenges—it is about choosing to see the good, even in the midst of difficulties.

This chapter will show you how to use gratitude as a daily healing tool to attract more joy, peace, and emotional resilience.

How Gratitude Heals Your Mind & Body

Science has proven what ancient wisdom has always taught: gratitude changes your brain.

- Studies show that practicing gratitude rewires neural pathways, increasing happiness and reducing stress.

- Gratitude releases dopamine and serotonin, the "feel-good" chemicals that promote emotional well-being.

- People who keep a gratitude practice experience better sleep, stronger immunity, and reduced anxiety.

When you express gratitude, you are not just thinking positively—you are shifting your energy field and attracting more of what you appreciate.

The Gratitude Healing Practice: A Step-by-Step Guide

If you are struggling with negativity, emotional pain, or stress, this guided gratitude practice will help you shift instantly.

Step 1: Breathe & Shift Your Awareness

Take a deep breath. Close your eyes and bring your focus to the present moment.

- Let go of any worries or distractions.
- Place your hand over your heart and feel your heartbeat.
- Recognize that you are alive, breathing, and capable of experiencing gratitude.

Step 2: Name Three Things You Are Grateful For

Say aloud or write down three things you are grateful for right now.

They can be small or big:

- The warmth of sunlight on your skin.
- A meaningful conversation you had today.
- The strength within you that has helped you overcome challenges.

Gratitude is most powerful when it is felt, not just listed. Take a moment to breathe in the feeling of appreciation.

Step 3: Reframe a Challenge with Gratitude

Gratitude is easy when things are going well. The real transformation happens when you can find gratitude even in difficult moments.

Think of a current challenge in your life. Ask yourself:

- What lesson is this experience teaching me?
- How is this situation helping me grow stronger?
- What hidden blessings might exist within this difficulty?

For example, instead of saying, *"I am struggling,"* you can say:

- *"I am grateful that this challenge is teaching me resilience."*
- *"I am grateful that I have the strength to overcome this."*
- *"I trust that something good is coming from this situation."*

By shifting your focus, you transform the energy around your struggles.

Step 4: Express Gratitude to Someone Else

One of the fastest ways to raise your vibration is by sharing gratitude with others.

- Send a message to someone thanking them for their support.
- Compliment a stranger or appreciate a loved one.
- Write a letter (or even just think about) someone who has positively impacted your life.

Gratitude multiplies when it is shared. The more you give, the more you receive.

Making Gratitude a Daily Habit

The key to unlocking gratitude's full power is consistency. Here are simple ways to integrate it into your daily life:

- **Morning Gratitude:** Start your day by listing three things you are grateful for.
- **Gratitude Walk:** Take a walk and mentally thank everything you see—trees, the sky, your own body for carrying you.
- **Gratitude Journal:** Write one sentence each night about what made you feel grateful that day.
- **Gratitude Before Sleep:** As you lie in bed, reflect on at least one moment from your day that brought you peace or joy.

The more you practice, the more gratitude becomes your natural state of being.

Final Thought: Gratitude is the Shortcut to Healing

Healing is not just about releasing pain—it is about making space for joy, love, and appreciation.

Gratitude is a bridge. It shifts your focus from what is missing to what is already present. And in that shift, healing happens.

Take a deep breath. Feel the abundance around you. Right now, in this moment, you have everything you need.

Seeing the Bigger Picture—How Self-Reflection Can Heal You

When you are in the middle of a challenge, it is easy to feel stuck, lost, or overwhelmed. Pain can make you believe that things will never change, that you are trapped in a cycle of suffering. But what if you could step back and see the bigger picture—the deeper meaning behind your experiences?

Self-reflection is a powerful healing tool. It helps you shift from asking, *"Why is this happening to me?"* to *"What is this teaching me?"*

When you learn to zoom out and see your life from a higher perspective, everything changes. You begin to realize that even the hardest moments carry wisdom, that the struggles you face are shaping you, and that healing is not about erasing the past but about understanding it differently.

Why Seeing the Bigger Picture Brings Healing

Pain often makes us focus on the immediate discomfort, blinding us to the long-term growth it can bring. But if you look at your past challenges, you will likely see that:

- Some of your biggest failures led to unexpected opportunities.
- The heartbreaks you endured taught you self-worth.
- The struggles you faced helped you build resilience.

Healing happens when you stop resisting your journey and start trusting it.

Every experience—good or bad—is part of a larger story. And when you begin to see it from a broader perspective, you stop feeling like a victim and start stepping into your own power.

The Self-Reflection Healing Exercise

If you are struggling to see the purpose behind a difficult situation, this practice will help you gain clarity, wisdom, and emotional release.

Step 1: Choose a Challenge You Are Facing

Take a moment to think about a recent experience that has been weighing on you. It could be:

- A loss or heartbreak.
- A failure or setback.
- A difficult decision you are struggling with.

Write it down in a journal or reflect on it in your mind.

Step 2: Shift from "Why?" to "What?"

Instead of asking:

- *"Why did this happen to me?"*
- *"Why do I always experience this pain?"*
- Shift your perspective and ask:
- "What is this teaching me?"
- "What strength am I developing because of this?"

- "What part of me needs healing that this experience is revealing?"

This simple shift in questioning moves you out of suffering and into awareness.

Step 3: Connect the Dots of Your Journey

Now, reflect on past struggles that seemed painful at the time but later made sense. Ask yourself:

- Have I overcome something similar before?
- How did that past challenge shape me in a positive way?
- Is it possible that this current situation is doing the same?

By looking at your past from a distance, you begin to see that challenges are not roadblocks—they are stepping stones.

Step 4: Reframe the Story

The way you tell your life story affects how you feel about yourself. If you constantly see yourself as someone who has been hurt, betrayed, or unlucky, that will be your experience. But if you shift your story, you shift your reality.

Try writing a new version of your story:

- **Instead of:** *"I was abandoned."* → **Say:** *"I was given an opportunity to learn self-reliance."*
- **Instead of:** *"I failed."* → **Say:** *"I was redirected toward something better."*
- **Instead of:** *"I was hurt."* → **Say:** *"I grew stronger and wiser through this experience."*

Your life is not happening to you. It is happening for you.

The Power of Perspective—Your Future Self Knows the Answer

If you could speak to your future self, five or ten years from now, what advice would they give you about this situation?

Your future self would likely tell you:

- *"This pain will pass."*
- *"You are learning something valuable."*
- *"Something better is waiting for you."*

By trusting this wisdom now, you accelerate your healing and stop carrying unnecessary emotional weight.

Final Thought: Trust the Journey

Healing does not mean avoiding pain—it means seeing it differently. When you step back and look at the bigger picture, you realize that life is guiding you, even when it does not seem like it.

Take a deep breath. Trust that one day, everything will make sense. You are exactly where you need to be.

Unfollow, Unfriend, Unsubscribe—Why Digital Detox is Self-Care

In today's world, we are constantly surrounded by digital noise—endless scrolling, notifications, news updates, and social media feeds filled with other people's lives. While technology has its benefits, it also distracts, drains, and overwhelms our minds with unnecessary information and energy.

Many people focus on detoxing their diet or lifestyle but forget about digital detoxing—cleansing their online space to protect their mental and emotional well-being.

If you have been feeling anxious, unmotivated, or mentally exhausted, this chapter will guide you through how to declutter your digital world and reclaim your peace.

How Digital Overload Affects Your Energy

Every time you pick up your phone, you expose yourself to an avalanche of external energy. Some of it is inspiring, but much of it is:

- **Unnecessary comparison** – Seeing curated versions of others' lives makes you feel like you are not doing enough.

- **Emotional manipulation** – Negative news, clickbait, and sensationalized content trigger fear and stress.

- **Mental clutter** – Constant notifications, messages, and online drama drain your focus.

- **Subconscious programming** – The more you engage with certain types of content, the more it shapes your beliefs, even without you realizing it.

Your mind and emotions absorb everything you consume—and if you are not intentional about what you allow in, it can create mental fog, low self-worth, and emotional exhaustion.

The Digital Detox Process: Clearing Out What No Longer Serves You

A digital detox does not mean you need to delete all social media or stop using technology altogether. It simply means choosing what deserves space in your energy field.

Step 1: Audit Your Online Environment

Take a moment to reflect on what you consume online. Ask yourself:

- Does this content uplift or drain me?

- Do I feel better or worse after scrolling?

- Am I following people out of inspiration or

obligation?

Be brutally honest. Your online space should feel like a safe, nourishing place—not an energy trap.

Step 2: Unfollow, Unfriend, Unsubscribe

Now, it is time to remove what no longer serves you.

- Unfollow accounts that make you feel insecure, anxious, or unworthy.

- Unfriend or mute people whose energy no longer aligns with yours.

- Unsubscribe from emails, pages, or groups that clutter your mind with unnecessary information.

Remember: It is not personal—it is self-care. You are not obligated to follow anyone who does not contribute positively to your energy.

Step 3: Set Boundaries with Technology

Social media and digital distractions are designed to consume your time and attention. To regain control:

- Turn off unnecessary notifications. Constant alerts keep your brain in a reactive state.

- Set screen time limits. Reduce mindless scrolling by giving yourself a fixed time for online activity.

- Create phone-free zones. Keep your mornings and evenings free from digital distractions.

- Schedule intentional breaks. Try one day a week without social media to reset your mind.

Your energy is precious. Do not let an algorithm control your emotions.

Step 4: Replace Digital Noise with Mindful Practices

Instead of automatically reaching for your phone, choose real-life activities that nourish your soul:

- Read a book that inspires growth.
- Journal your thoughts instead of scrolling through others' opinions.
- Spend time in nature without distractions.
- Have meaningful, in-person conversations.
- Meditate or practice deep breathing for inner clarity.

By filling your life with intentional activities, you naturally lose the urge to seek validation or stimulation from your screen.

Reclaiming Your Peace in a Digital World

The more intentional you become about your online space, the more mentally clear, emotionally stable, and spiritually grounded you will feel.

Technology is a tool—use it wisely, instead of letting it use you.

Right now, take a deep breath. You do not need to consume everything. You have the power to choose peace.

Spiritual Practices for Inner Peace—Meditation, Prayer & Stillness

In the rush of daily life, it is easy to get caught up in stress, distractions, and external noise. But true peace is not found in the outside world—it is cultivated from within.

Spiritual practices like meditation, prayer, and stillness are not just religious rituals; they are tools for healing, grounding, and reconnecting with your highest self.

When practiced consistently, they help you:

- Calm an overactive mind.
- Detach from external chaos.
- Strengthen your inner guidance and intuition.

- Heal emotional wounds and raise your energy.

You do not need to follow a specific belief system or have hours of free time. Even a few moments of daily spiritual practice can create profound shifts.

The Three Pillars of Spiritual Peace: Meditation, Prayer & Stillness

Each of these practices offers a unique way to connect with yourself, the universe, or a higher power.

- Meditation – A practice of quieting the mind and expanding awareness.

- Prayer – A sacred conversation with the universe, God, or your higher self.

- Stillness – A deep presence in the moment, allowing peace to naturally arise.

Choose the one that resonates most with you—or combine them for a more powerful effect.

1. Meditation—Quieting the Mind, Expanding Awareness

Meditation is not about stopping thoughts—it is about detaching from them. It teaches you that you are not your thoughts, fears, or worries—you are the awareness behind them.

The Simple Meditation Practice for Healing

- Find a quiet space. Sit comfortably, close your eyes, and take a deep breath.

- Focus on your breath. Inhale slowly through your nose, exhale gently through your mouth.

- Observe your thoughts without attachment. If a thought arises, do not resist it. Simply let it pass like a cloud in the sky.

- Allow stillness to grow. As you continue, you will notice a deep sense of peace unfolding within you.

Even 5–10 minutes a day of meditation can reduce stress, enhance clarity, and bring emotional balance.

2. Prayer—Speaking with the Universe

Prayer is not about religious dogma—it is about connection. It is an intimate conversation with the universe, God, or your higher self.

How to Pray for Healing & Guidance

- **Gratitude Prayer:** Instead of asking for things, thank the universe for what you already have. This shifts your energy to abundance.

- **Surrender Prayer:** If you feel overwhelmed, say: *"I release control and trust that everything is unfolding for my highest good."*

- **Intention Prayer:** Speak your desires into existence with conviction. *"I am ready to receive love, peace, and healing."*

Prayer does not have to follow a script. Speak from your heart. The universe always listens.

3. The Power of Stillness—Returning to the Present Moment

Many people seek peace through external actions, but true peace comes when you simply stop and allow yourself to just be.

Stillness is about learning to sit with yourself without distractions. It is the most overlooked yet deeply transformative spiritual practice.

How to Practice Stillness

- Pause for a moment. Put down your phone, step away from distractions.

- Breathe and feel your surroundings. Notice the sounds, the sensations in your body.

- Let go of the need to do anything. Just be. Observe. Exist in the now.

When you practice stillness, you create space for answers, healing, and clarity to naturally arise.

Making Spiritual Practices a Daily Habit

You do not need an elaborate routine—just a few intentional moments each day.

- **Morning:** Start your day with gratitude or a short meditation.

- **Throughout the Day:** Pause and practice deep breaths whenever you feel overwhelmed.

- **Evening:** End your day with a simple prayer or a few moments of stillness.

The more you practice, the more inner peace becomes your natural state.

Final Thought: Peace is Already Within You

You do not have to seek peace outside of yourself. It is already inside you, waiting to be uncovered.

Meditation, prayer, and stillness are simply pathways that help you return to it.

Take a deep breath. Feel the silence beneath the noise. You are already whole.

Color Therapy—How Colors Affect Your Mood & Energy

Colors are more than just visual aesthetics—they carry energy, influence emotions, and even impact your physical well-being. From ancient healing traditions to modern psychology, color therapy has been used to restore balance, uplift the mind, and promote healing.

Have you ever felt instantly calm when looking at a soft blue sky? Or energized by the sight of bright yellow flowers? This is because colors have the power to shift your energy field.

If you are feeling emotionally drained, unmotivated, or stuck in negative thought patterns, using color therapy consciously can bring a profound shift in your mood, focus, and overall well-being.

The Science & Energy of Colors

Every color carries a specific vibration that affects your emotions, mind, and energy field. Research in color psychology has shown that different shades can:

- Boost mood and creativity (yellow, orange)
- Promote relaxation and calmness (blue, green)
- Increase motivation and confidence (red, gold)
- Encourage emotional healing and self-love (pink, violet)

By understanding how colors influence your state of being, you can intentionally use them to support your healing journey.

How to Use Color Therapy for Healing

You do not need expensive tools or formal training to benefit from color therapy. Simple changes in your environment, wardrobe, and visualization practices can shift your energy.

1. Wear Colors That Match Your Intention

Your clothes carry energy. The colors you wear influence your mood, mindset, and even how others perceive you.

Need confidence & strength? Wear red to boost motivation and courage.

Seeking peace & relaxation? Choose blue or white for a calming effect.

Feeling emotionally blocked? Use green to open your heart to healing.

Want to enhance intuition? Try purple to connect with deeper wisdom.

If you feel drawn to a certain color, trust that your energy already knows what it needs.

2. Surround Yourself with Healing Colors

The colors in your environment directly affect your emotions. Use them intentionally:

- **Home Décor:** Bring in colors that create the atmosphere you desire—soft blues in the bedroom for relaxation, energizing oranges in creative spaces, or grounding earthy tones for stability.

- **Lighting:** Using warm yellow or golden lights in the evening helps create a sense of coziness and emotional warmth.

- **Crystals & Objects:** Placing colored objects (like candles, fabrics, or paintings) in your space can help shift energy.

Your surroundings should support the emotions and energy you want to cultivate.

3. Use Color Visualization for Energy Healing

One of the most powerful ways to absorb color energy is through visualization.

Try this simple Color Healing Meditation:

I. Close your eyes and take a deep breath.

II. Imagine a soft, glowing light surrounding your body.

III. Choose a color that represents what you need.

- Golden light for confidence.
- Green light for emotional healing.
- Blue light for mental clarity and peace.
- Pink light for self-love and compassion.

4. **Visualize this color filling your entire being, dissolving any stress, sadness, or heaviness.**

5. **Breathe deeply and affirm:**

   - *"I am absorbing the energy of healing and renewal."*

This practice instantly calms your mind, balances your energy, and helps realign your emotions.

Color Therapy & Chakras—Aligning Your Energy Centers

In ancient healing traditions, colors are associated with chakras—energy centers in the body.

If you feel off-balance, using the corresponding color can help:

- **Root Chakra (Red):** Grounding, stability, overcoming fear.
- **Sacral Chakra (Orange):** Creativity, passion, emotional flow.
- **Solar Plexus (Yellow):** Confidence, personal power, motivation.
- **Heart Chakra (Green or Pink):** Love, forgiveness, emotional healing.
- **Throat Chakra (Blue):** Communication, self-expression, truth.
- **Third Eye (Indigo):** Intuition, inner wisdom, deep focus.
- **Crown Chakra (Violet or White):** Spiritual connection, higher consciousness.

If a specific area of your life feels blocked, wear, meditate on, or surround yourself with that color to restore balance.

Final Thought: Let Colors Heal You

Color therapy is one of the simplest yet most effective ways to influence your mood, energy, and healing process. You do not need to do anything complex—just invite the right colors into your daily life and let them work their magic.

Right now, take a deep breath and look around you. What colors are speaking to you today?

Listen to them. They are guiding you toward balance, healing, and renewal.

Who You Spend Time With Matters—How to Choose the Right People

The people around you are not just companions—they are energy influencers. Every conversation, every interaction, every shared moment is an exchange of energy. Some people lift you up, inspire you, and help you grow. Others drain you, trigger old wounds, or keep you stuck in unhealthy patterns.

Your healing journey is deeply influenced by who you allow into your space. If you want to feel lighter, more at peace, and aligned with your best self, you must be mindful of the company you keep.

This chapter will help you identify which relationships support your growth and which ones hold you back—so you can surround yourself with people who nurture your healing.

The Energy of Relationships—Why It Affects Your Healing

Every relationship has an energetic impact on your life. Some people pour love and light into you, while others unknowingly (or knowingly) drain your energy.

Think about the people you interact with regularly. Ask yourself:

- Do I feel lighter or heavier after spending time with them?

- Do they encourage my healing and growth, or keep me stuck in old patterns?

- Do they genuinely support my happiness, or only tolerate me when I fit into their expectations?

The answers to these questions reveal who belongs in your life and who may be blocking your healing.

The Three Types of People in Your Life

1. The Supporters—Your Soul Tribe

These are the people who:

- Celebrate your growth.

- Listen without judgment.

- Encourage your healing and self-improvement.

- Bring peace, positivity, and wisdom into your life.

Keep these people close. They are the ones who truly see you and uplift your journey.

2. The Drainers—Energy Vampires

These are people who:

- Constantly complain, criticize, or bring negativity.

- Make everything about themselves, never listening to you.

- Subtly (or openly) discourage your healing and self-improvement.

- Leave you feeling exhausted, anxious, or unworthy.

These relationships often feel obligatory rather than joyful. Pay attention to how your body feels around them—if you feel drained, it is time to set boundaries.

3. The In-Betweeners—People Who Are Neither Good Nor Bad

Some relationships are neutral. These people are not harmful, but they also do not contribute positively to your healing. They may be acquaintances, old friends, or family members you interact with out of habit rather than deep connection.

Ask yourself: Do I truly enjoy this person's presence, or am I maintaining this relationship out of obligation?

If the connection no longer aligns, it is okay to create distance.

How to Protect Your Energy & Choose the Right People

If you want to heal, grow, and evolve, your relationships must reflect that.

Step 1: Reduce Time with Toxic Influences

Not everyone deserves access to your energy. If someone consistently drains you, limit your time with them.

- Stop engaging in negative conversations.

- Decline invitations that feel like an obligation.

- Set emotional boundaries—do not let their energy affect your peace.

Step 2: Set Clear Boundaries

If someone repeatedly disrespects your boundaries or triggers your emotional wounds, it is time to establish clear limits.

You can say:

- "I need to focus on my healing right now and will be stepping back from certain interactions."
- "I value my peace, so I am choosing to limit my exposure to negativity."
- "I am no longer available for conversations that bring me down."

Boundaries are not rude—they are self-care.

Step 3: Find & Attract Your Soul-Aligned People

The more you grow, the more you will naturally attract people who align with your energy.

Ways to invite supportive people into your life:

- Join communities that match your interests (spiritual groups, creative circles, wellness spaces).
- Seek relationships based on authenticity, not convenience.
- Let go of toxic relationships so new ones can enter your life.

Energy attracts energy. When you embody the qualities you seek in others, the right people will find you.

Final Thought: You Deserve to Be Surrounded by Love

Healing is not just about self-work—it is also about choosing relationships that nurture your soul.

You do not have to tolerate people who bring chaos, insecurity, or negativity into your life. You have the right to protect your energy, walk away, and surround yourself with those who truly support your healing.

Take a deep breath. You are allowed to choose peace. You are allowed to choose love.

Talking to a Healer—When & Why You Might Need Professional Help

Healing is a journey, and while self-healing practices are powerful, there are times when seeking guidance from a professional healer can create a deeper, more transformative shift.

Some wounds are layered. Some traumas are deeply embedded. Some emotional struggles persist despite your best efforts. In such cases, working with an experienced healer can help you break through blocks, release stored pain, and accelerate your growth.

This chapter explores when and why seeking professional healing support is beneficial, what types of healers exist, and how to find the right one for your journey.

Signs That You May Benefit from a Healer's Guidance

While self-healing is essential, it is not always enough. Sometimes, external support is needed to uncover hidden wounds, process emotions, and move past deeply rooted blocks.

Ask yourself:

- Have I been struggling with the same emotional pain for a long time?

- Do I feel stuck, even after trying different healing techniques?

- Am I carrying trauma or suppressed emotions that feel too overwhelming to face alone?

- Do I feel disconnected from myself, my emotions, or my spiritual path?

- Have I experienced major loss, grief, or life changes that feel too heavy to process?

If you resonate with any of these, a healer can help you navigate through your healing journey with more clarity and support.

Types of Healers & Modalities—Finding What Works for You

Not all healing is the same. Different healing methods work for different people. It is important to find what resonates with you.

1. Energy Healers—Clearing Emotional & Spiritual Blocks

If you feel emotionally heavy, drained, or stuck in old patterns, energy healing can help you release blocked energy and restore balance.

- **Reiki Healing** – Uses universal life force energy to cleanse emotional, physical, and spiritual imbalances.

- **Pranic Healing** – Works with the body's energy field to clear emotional and mental blockages.

- **Chakra Balancing** – Aligns and heals the body's energy centers for overall well-being.

Best for: Emotional healing, stress relief, and energetic detox.

2. Trauma & Emotional Release Therapists

For those dealing with deep-seated pain, trauma, or unresolved past experiences, working with a trained therapist or trauma healer can bring profound relief.

- **Somatic Therapy** – Focuses on releasing trauma stored in the body.

- **EMDR (Eye Movement Desensitization and Reprocessing)** – Helps process and heal past traumatic memories.

- **Hypnotherapy** – Reprograms subconscious beliefs and heals emotional wounds.

Best for: Processing deep emotional pain, PTSD, and breaking destructive patterns.

2. Spiritual Guides & Intuitive Healers

If you feel disconnected from your purpose, lost in life, or spiritually stuck, a spiritual healer can help you reconnect with your higher self.

- **Shamans** – Work with ancient healing practices to clear karmic imprints and soul-level wounds.

- **Akashic Record Readers** – Access your soul's history to provide guidance on your life path.

- **Past Life Regression Therapists** – Help uncover and heal past-life traumas affecting your present.

Best for: Spiritual awakening, soul healing, and deep clarity on life's purpose.

3. Holistic Therapists for Mind-Body Healing

If your emotional struggles are manifesting as physical symptoms (chronic pain, anxiety, digestive issues), holistic healers bridge the mind-body connection.

- **Ayurvedic Practitioners** – Use ancient medicine to heal emotional and physical imbalances.

- **Traditional Chinese Medicine (TCM) Healers** – Balance the body's energy using acupuncture, herbal remedies, and Qi healing.

- **Sound Healing Therapists** – Use frequencies and vibrations to restore harmony in the body.

Best for: Healing physical symptoms caused by emotional stress and restoring mind-body balance.

How to Find the Right Healer for You

With so many healing options available, how do you choose the right healer?

1. **Trust Your Intuition** – The right healer will resonate with you. If something feels "off," keep searching.

2. **Ask for Recommendations** – Seek referrals from

trusted friends, spiritual mentors, or wellness communities.

3. **Research Their Methods & Approach** – Read about their work, testimonials, and healing philosophy.

4. **Book an Initial Consultation** – Most healers offer a short introductory session—this helps you feel if their energy aligns with yours.

5. **Observe How You Feel After the Session** – A good healer leaves you feeling empowered, lighter, and more connected to yourself.

Remember, no healer can "fix" you—they simply guide you to activate your own healing power.

Healing Is a Collaborative Process

Seeing a healer does not mean you are weak—it means you are committed to your growth. Healing is not about relying on someone else; it is about receiving the right support to accelerate your own journey.

A true healer does not create dependency. Instead, they empower you to reconnect with your inner strength, wisdom, and self-healing abilities.

Final Thought: You Are Your Own Healer, But You Do Not Have to Walk Alone

Seeking healing support is not a sign of weakness; it is an act of self-love. Whether you choose energy work, therapy, spiritual guidance, or holistic healing, what matters is that you choose yourself.

Trusting the Universe—How to Let Go & Believe in Divine Timing

There are moments in life when things do not go as planned. You try, you push, you struggle—and yet, the results do not come. In these moments, frustration builds, fear takes over, and doubt creeps in.

But what if the universe is not working against you? What if delays, detours, and setbacks are actually redirections toward something better?

Trusting the universe is not about waiting passively. It is about letting go of control, surrendering the need for instant answers, and believing that everything is unfolding exactly as it should.

This chapter will guide you through how to trust divine timing, release resistance, and open yourself to the magic of life.

Why Letting Go Is the Key to Peace

Many people struggle with trust because they feel they need to control everything in order to be safe. But control is an illusion—life will always bring unexpected changes. The more you resist, the more you suffer.

When you learn to surrender, you:

- Stop fighting reality and allow life to flow.
- Release stress and anxiety about things beyond your control.
- Create space for unexpected miracles and opportunities.
- Feel lighter, freer, and more at peace.

Surrender does not mean giving up—it means trusting that the universe knows what is best for you.

The Three Signs the Universe Is Guiding You

Even when you do not see it, the universe is always sending signs. If you pay attention, you will realize that life is constantly guiding you.

1. Delays & Closed Doors

If something is not working out despite your best efforts, it may not be meant for you right now.

- A job you did not get, a relationship that ended, an opportunity that fell through—these are not failures. They are redirects.

- Instead of asking "Why is this happening to me?", ask "What is this protecting me from?"

2. Repeated Patterns & Lessons

If the same situation keeps repeating in your life, it is a sign that there is a lesson you have not yet learned.

- Are you attracting the same type of relationships?

- Are you facing similar financial struggles?

- Are you experiencing cycles of self-doubt?

These are not coincidences—they are opportunities for healing. Once you understand the lesson, the pattern will break.

3. Synchronicities & Intuitive Nudges

When you are in alignment with the universe, signs start appearing everywhere.

- Seeing repeated numbers (11:11, 222, 777).

- Running into the right person at the right time.

- Feeling an inner pull to change directions.

These signs confirm that you are on the right path—even if you cannot see the full picture yet.

How to Strengthen Your Trust in the Universe

Trust is a practice. If you struggle with doubt, these simple steps will help you build faith and let go of fear.

Step 1: Release the Need to Control Everything

When you try to control every detail of life, you block the natural flow of miracles. Instead, say:

"I surrender the need to control. I trust that what is meant for me will come at the right time."

Breathe deeply and feel the relief of letting go.

Step 2: Ask for Guidance, Then Let It Go

If you need clarity, ask the universe for a sign. You can say:

- *"Show me a sign that I am on the right path."*
- *"If this is meant for me, let it flow easily. If not, guide me elsewhere."*

Then, stop obsessing. Let the answer come naturally.

Step 3: Focus on the Present Moment

Worrying about the future does not change it. Trusting the universe means fully embracing where you are right now.

- If you are waiting for a dream to manifest, enjoy the journey.
- If you are healing from the past, be patient with the process.
- If something feels uncertain, remind yourself:

"Everything is unfolding exactly as it should."

Final Thought: The Universe Has a Plan for You

When things do not go as expected, trust that life is working in your favor. Every delay, every redirection, every unanswered prayer is leading you to something greater than you can imagine.

Take a deep breath. You are supported. You are exactly where you need to be.

Manifesting Miracles—How to Rewrite Your Story with Faith

Miracles are not rare occurrences—they happen every day, all around you. The problem is, most people do not recognize them because they are too focused on what is missing, what is wrong, or what has not yet manifested.

But here is the truth: You are not just a passive observer in your life—you are a creator. Your thoughts, beliefs, and energy shape your reality. The moment you shift your mindset, open yourself to possibility, and align with the flow of the universe, miracles become inevitable.

This chapter will teach you how to step into the energy of miracles and manifest a life that aligns with your highest self.

What Is a Miracle? (And Why They Are Closer Than You Think)

Most people think of miracles as supernatural, impossible events. But in reality, a miracle is simply a shift in perception and energy that allows something extraordinary to unfold.

A miracle can be:

- Finding exactly what you need at the perfect time.

- Healing from emotional pain you thought would last forever.

- Receiving an unexpected opportunity that changes your life.

- Overcoming a challenge with strength you did not know you had.

Miracles are not about luck—they are about alignment. When you change the way you see the world, the world changes for you.

How to Manifest Miracles in Your Life

If you are ready to open yourself to miracles, follow these steps to shift your energy and allow divine possibilities to unfold.

Step 1: Believe That Miracles Are Possible

The first step to manifesting miracles is simple: You must believe they can happen.

Doubt is a block. If you constantly tell yourself, "Things never work out for me," or "Miracles only happen for other people," then that becomes your reality.

Instead, affirm daily:

- *"I am open to receiving miracles."*
- *"Unexpected blessings flow into my life with ease."*
- *"The universe is always working in my favor."*

What you believe, you create.

Step 2: Shift from Fear to Trust

Many people block their own blessings because they are trapped in fear, doubt, and control. The universe cannot deliver miracles if you are energetically closed off.

- Instead of fearing the worst, expect the best.
- Instead of worrying, trust that what is meant for you is already on its way.
- Instead of resisting change, embrace it as part of your growth.

When you let go of fear, you make space for the extraordinary to unfold.

Step 3: Align Your Energy with What You Desire

You do not attract what you want—you attract what you are.

If you want love, become a person who radiates love.

If you want success, embody confidence and worthiness.

If you want peace, practice stillness and gratitude.

The universe mirrors your energy. When you embody the feelings and mindset of the reality you desire, you naturally attract it.

Try this:

- Visualize yourself already living your dream life.
- Feel the emotions of having it—joy, gratitude, excitement.
- Act as if it is already happening.

This energy shift creates a magnetic pull that draws miracles to you.

Step 4: Let Go & Allow the Universe to Work

The final step is often the hardest: surrender.

Manifesting miracles is not about forcing things to happen—it is about aligning with divine timing. Sometimes, the universe has a bigger plan than you can see.

Let go of the 'how' and 'when.'

- If something does not manifest immediately, trust that it is coming in the perfect way at the perfect time.
- If you face a challenge, know that it is part of your preparation for something greater.

Faith is not about seeing—it is about knowing that what you desire is already on its way.

Final Thought: You Are a Magnet for Miracles

Right now, as you read this, miracles are already being prepared for you. The universe is aligning circumstances, guiding people toward you, and opening doors you have not even imagined.

Take a deep breath.

Trust.

The miracles you seek are already on their way.

Building a Healing Routine—A Simple Daily Plan for Lifelong Peace

Healing is not a one-time event. It is a lifelong process of nurturing yourself, clearing old energy, and making conscious choices that align with your highest well-being.

Many people experience moments of deep healing but then slip back into old patterns because they do not have a daily structure to support their growth.

The secret to lasting healing is not in occasional breakthroughs—it is in consistent, daily habits that renew your mind, body, and spirit.

This chapter will help you create a simple, sustainable healing routine that keeps you balanced, grounded, and emotionally strong—every single day.

Why a Healing Routine is Essential

Imagine healing as building a foundation for a peaceful life.

- Without daily reinforcement, old wounds, stress, and emotional triggers can creep back in.
- With a healing routine, you create stability, emotional resilience, and a deep sense of inner peace.

The best part? Healing does not have to be complicated. Small, intentional habits each day can lead to powerful transformation.

The Daily Healing Routine—A Step-by-Step Guide

You do not need hours of spiritual practice. A simple

morning, midday, and evening healing routine can be enough to shift your entire life.

1. Morning Healing Ritual—Set the Tone for the Day

How you start your morning shapes your mindset, energy, and emotions for the entire day. Instead of reaching for your phone or diving into stress, try this:

Step 1: Mindful Awakening – As soon as you wake up, take a deep breath and place your hand on your heart. Affirm:

"Today, I choose peace. I welcome healing into my life."

Step 2: Energy Cleansing – Splash your face with cold water or take a warm shower, imagining the water washing away any stagnant energy.

Step 3: Gratitude & Intention Setting – List three things you are grateful for and set a positive intention for the day. Example:

"I choose to focus on joy today."

Step 4: Movement & Breathwork – Stretch your body, take a few deep breaths, or do a short walk to awaken your energy.

Step 5: Protective Energy Shield – Close your eyes and visualize a golden light surrounding you, protecting you from negativity throughout the day.

This 5–10 minute morning routine will ground you in peace and strength before the world pulls you in different directions.

2. Midday Healing Reset—Recenter & Release Stress

Life can be chaotic. By midday, stress, distractions, and external energy can start to weigh you down. Take a few minutes to reset:

Step 1: Breathe & Check In – Close your eyes and take three deep breaths. Ask yourself: How am I feeling right now?

Step 2: Release Tension – If you feel anxious or drained, shake out your hands, stretch, or place your palms over your heart and breathe.

Step 3: Energy Detox Affirmation – Whisper to yourself:

"I release all energy that does not belong to me. I reclaim my peace."

Step 4: Hydration & Grounding – Drink a glass of water and take a few moments to feel present in your body.

This quick midday reset helps clear negative energy and realign your focus.

3. Evening Healing Ritual—Let Go & Recharge

Before bed, it is crucial to release the energy of the day so you do not carry stress into your subconscious.

Step 1: Emotional Release – Write down any thoughts, worries, or emotions that surfaced during the day.

(Example: "Today, I felt frustrated about ____. I release this now.")

Step 2: Energy Cleansing Shower – Take a shower or a salt bath, visualizing negativity washing away.

Step 3: Gratitude Reflection – Think of one good thing that happened today, no matter how small.

Step 4: Silent Stillness or Meditation – Sit in silence for a few moments, allowing yourself to rest in pure presence.

Step 5: Sleep Intention – Before sleeping, whisper:

"I release this day. I allow my body, mind, and soul to heal as I sleep."

This nighttime healing ritual ensures you end the day with peace and renewal.

Bonus Healing Practices to Add to Your Routine

You can personalize your routine by incorporating other healing tools that resonate with you:

- **Journaling** – Writing helps process emotions and gain clarity.

- **Spiritual Practices** – Prayer, meditation, or chanting for deeper connection.

- **Nature Connection** – Walking barefoot, sitting under a tree, or watching the sunset.

- **Creative Expression** – Painting, singing, or dancing to express emotions freely.

- **Reading or Listening to Wisdom** – Spiritual books, affirmations, or uplifting podcasts.

The key is consistency. Even small practices, done daily, create lasting healing.

Final Thought: Healing is a Lifestyle, Not a Destination

True healing does not happen in one big breakthrough—it happens in the small choices you make every day.

By creating a daily healing routine, you:

- Keep your mind clear.

- Keep your emotions balanced.

- Keep your energy strong and protected.

Take a deep breath. You are becoming the most healed, peaceful, and powerful version of yourself—one day at a time.

How Spirituality Heals—The Connection Between Faith & Well-being

Healing is not just about the body or the mind—it is about the soul. Many people try to heal through therapy, self-help techniques, and physical practices, but something still feels missing. That missing piece is often a spiritual connection.

Spirituality is not about religion or rituals—it is about faith, surrender, and connecting with something greater than yourself. When you bring spirituality into your healing journey, you gain clarity, peace, and a deep inner strength that cannot be shaken.

This chapter explores how spirituality accelerates healing, relieves emotional burdens, and restores balance to your life.

Why Spirituality is a Powerful Healer

Science now confirms what ancient wisdom has always known: faith, prayer, and spiritual connection have measurable healing effects.

- People who have a strong spiritual practice experience lower stress levels, faster recovery from illness, and greater emotional resilience.

- Spirituality gives meaning to suffering, helping people see challenges as part of their soul's growth rather than random misfortunes.

- Faith in a higher power reduces anxiety and fear, providing comfort even in uncertain times.

You do not have to follow a strict religious path—all you need is an openness to something beyond yourself.

How Spirituality Heals the Mind, Body & Soul

If you feel lost, disconnected, or stuck in pain, spiritual practices can help you find clarity and inner peace. Here is how:

1. Faith Shifts Your Perspective on Pain

When you believe that life is happening for you, not to you, suffering no longer feels meaningless.

- Instead of thinking, *"Why is this happening to me?"*, faith allows you to ask, *"What is this teaching me?"*
- You begin to trust that every challenge is guiding you toward greater wisdom and strength.

Pain does not disappear, but it becomes easier to carry when you trust there is a purpose behind it.

2. Prayer & Surrender Relieve Emotional Burdens

Many people struggle because they try to carry everything alone—their fears, worries, and struggles.

Prayer is not about asking for miracles—it is about surrendering what is too heavy to hold alone.

A simple prayer for healing:

"I release my worries, fears, and pain to the universe (or God). I trust that everything is being taken care of in divine timing. I surrender and allow healing to flow into my life."

Even if you do not follow a religious path, speaking your heart's burdens aloud helps release emotional weight.

3. Meditation & Stillness Open You to Divine Guidance

Spiritual healing is not just about asking—it is also about listening. When you sit in silence, you allow wisdom to flow to you.

Try this:

- Find a quiet space.
- Close your eyes and take a deep breath.
- Instead of thinking, simply be still and listen.

The more you practice, the more you will receive intuitive insights, inner clarity, and a deep sense of peace.

4. Spirituality Reconnects You to Love & Unity

One of the biggest causes of suffering is the feeling of separation—from others, from life, from yourself.

Spirituality reminds you that you are never alone.

- You are connected to a higher power.

- You are connected to every living being.

- You are part of something much greater than yourself.

This realization dissolves loneliness, fear, and isolation. You begin to feel supported, guided, and at peace.

Simple Spiritual Practices for Daily Healing

You do not need to follow religious traditions to experience spiritual healing. Choose what resonates with you:

- **Morning Prayer or Gratitude** – Start your day by speaking to the universe and giving thanks.

- **Meditation or Deep Breathing** – Sit in silence to receive guidance and clarity.

- **Nature Connection** – Spend time in nature to feel the presence of something greater.

- **Acts of Kindness & Service** – Giving love to others brings healing back to you.

- **Trust & Letting Go** – Release the need for control and allow life to flow naturally.

The more you nurture your spiritual connection, the more peace, clarity, and healing will naturally flow into your life.

Final Thought: Trust the Unseen, Heal from Within

Spirituality does not mean escaping reality—it means embracing life with trust, love, and openness. When you believe in something beyond yourself, healing becomes effortless.

BECOMING A HEALER: TRANSFORM YOUR PAIN INTO PURPOSE

Becoming a Healer—How to Turn Your Healing Into a Career

This part of the book is deeply personal to me because it aligns with my mission—One healer in every house. Imagine a world where every family has at least one person who understands energy, emotions, and transformation. A world where healing is not just an occasional practice, but a way of life.

If you have reached this part of the book, it means you are ready to take healing to the next level. And this next level is exceptionally magical.

The Journey of a Professional Healer

Every healer's path is unique, but there is a common pattern that unfolds for those who truly commit to this journey. If you are feeling called to step into healing as a career, here is what the journey typically looks like:

1. **The Calling:** You bump into healing—perhaps through a personal experience, a book, or a sudden life event that shifts your awareness.

2. **The Curiosity Phase:** You begin implementing a few techniques and start seeing the magic of transformation in your own life.

3. **The Deep Healing:** You work on yourself, clearing emotional wounds, shifting energy, and experiencing profound breakthroughs.

4. **The Learning Stage:** You seek deeper knowledge and start learning multiple healing modalities such as chakras, aura cleansing, karmic healing, angel work, Reiki, EFT, and more.

5. **Healing Close Circles:** You start using these techniques on family and friends, seeing their lives change as a result of your work.

6. **Professional Expansion:** You begin offering your services to others, charging for your expertise, and gaining confidence as a healer.

7. **Scaling Up:** You refine your skills, expand your reach, and build a sustainable, profitable healing practice.

8. **Becoming a Super Healer:** You not only heal individuals but also train others, making a massive impact while building a life of purpose, success, and abundance.

If you want to take this path forward and convert healing into a thriving coaching business, getting in touch with the right mentor or healing coach is crucial. A guide who has walked this path before can help you accelerate your growth and lay the right foundation for your journey.

The Importance of the Right Coach

A skilled coach hand-holds you through the process, ensuring you understand both the science and the art of healing. When people approach you with their struggles, your ability to diagnose and guide them correctly is what separates an amateur from a professional. Two things are essential in this process:

1. **Confidentiality** – A healer holds a sacred space where people feel safe sharing their deepest wounds. Trust is everything.

2. **Root Cause Diagnosis** – Most problems seen on the surface are symptoms of deeper blockages. A trained healer knows how to detect and address the true source of the issue.

With the right training, you will master the skill of diagnosis and implement the right healing modalities in the right combination for amplified results.

Blending Logic & Magic—The Secret to Effective Healing

The best healers integrate both science (logic) and energy (magic). Healing is not just about intuition or spiritual tools—it is also about understanding psychology, human behavior, and the subtle workings of energy.

- **Logic:** This is the structured, scientific part—understanding how healing modalities work, the psychology of emotions, and how energy imbalances manifest in real life.

- **Magic:** This is the energetic part—the unseen shifts, the transformations that happen at a soul level when you apply healing techniques correctly.

A healer who understands both logic and magic creates extraordinary results. They don't just give temporary relief; they create lasting change.

Next Step: Answering the Call

If you feel drawn to not just heal yourself but heal others, this is your moment to step forward. The world needs more healers. People are searching for guides who can help them break free from pain, uncertainty, and emotional distress.

Your healing journey is not just for you. It is meant to be shared. And when you step into this path with intention, dedication, and the right knowledge, you become unstoppable...

Sharing the Gift—Helping Others & Creating a Ripple Effect

Healing is not just about your own transformation—it is about how your healing radiates into the world. Healing is energy, and like a drop in still water, it creates ripples far beyond what the eye can see. When you commit to your own growth, your presence alone becomes an unspoken message to those around you. You are already a healer, even before you teach, guide, or help others.

But here is the secret: The real magic happens when you share your healing. Not in grand gestures, but in the way you show up in the world, in the energy you carry, in the quiet moments of connection that spark transformation in others without you even realizing it.

The Silent Impact of Your Energy

Healing is not always about words—it is about who you become.

Have you ever noticed how being around someone deeply at peace makes you feel calm? Or how someone who radiates positivity uplifts an entire room? This is the silent impact of energy.

When you heal yourself, you naturally influence others:

- Your peace becomes contagious.
- Your presence becomes a safe space for others.
- Your authenticity inspires others to drop their masks.
- Your energy reminds people that healing is possible.

And the most beautiful part? You don't have to "do" anything special—your very being is the gift.

The Three Phases of Healing & Giving

There are three stages in how healing extends beyond yourself:

1. **Healing Yourself** – The personal transformation stage, where you do the inner work and experience deep breakthroughs.

2. **Healing by Example** – Without realizing it, you become a guide simply by living in alignment. People start noticing the change in you and ask, "What are you doing differently?"

3. **Healing as a Service** – This is when you consciously step into the role of a guide, teacher, or healer, actively supporting others in their journey.

Every healer begins as the wounded, and through their own healing, they awaken others. Healing is never meant to be contained—it is meant to flow.

The Ripple Effect: Changing Lives Without Realizing It

There are many ways to share your healing. Some are obvious—through coaching, energy healing, or teaching. But some are unexpected, subtle, and just as powerful.

- A stranger watches how you handle a difficult moment with grace and learns something valuable.

- A friend remembers a single sentence you once said, and it changes how they see themselves.

- Someone reads your words, listens to your story, or experiences your energy—and their own healing begins.

The truth is, you never truly know how far your healing reaches. And that is what makes it so magical.

The Mission: A Healer in Every Home—Changing the World, One Soul at a Time

Imagine a world where healing is not something rare, but something woven into everyday life.

Imagine if, in every home, there was at least one person who could hold space for emotions, clear energy, and guide their family through life's challenges with wisdom and love.

What if healing was not something people searched for later in life, after years of pain, but something taught and embraced from the beginning?

This is not a fantasy—it is a movement. And it starts with you.

Power of a Healer in Every Home

- A healer in every home means children growing up emotionally aware and energetically balanced.

- It means families handling stress with love, not conflict.

- It means breaking generational cycles of trauma.

- It means a world where healing is not just for a select few, but for everyone.

When you heal, you shift the energy of your family, your relationships, your lineage. This is how real change begins—not through governments or policies, but through the hearts and energy of people.

How You Can Be the Healer in Your Home

Healing does not mean you have to be a coach, a spiritual teacher, or a professional healer. It simply means you commit to being a source of light, wisdom, and peace in your home.

Ways to be the healer in your home:

- Create a space where emotions are welcome, not suppressed.

- Teach your loved ones about the power of energy, mindfulness, and self-awareness.

- Show, by example, how to navigate life's challenges with strength and grace.

- Hold space for healing—whether through deep conversations, energy work, or simply your presence.

- Break patterns of fear, lack, and unworthiness by embodying self-love and confidence.

You do not need to "fix" anyone. You simply need to be the change.

A Personal Invitation: The Time is Now

Healing is no longer something meant for the few—it is meant for the many. The world is shifting, consciousness is rising, and now, more than ever, healers are needed.

If you have felt this calling within you, this is your time to step forward.

Not everyone will understand this path. Not everyone will be ready. But that is okay—because the right people will be drawn to your energy, to your presence, to your light.

This is bigger than just healing yourself. This is about awakening the world, one person, one home, one family at a time.

And it starts with you.

Final Thought: You Are the Beginning of This Movement

You do not need permission to be a healer.

You do not need to be perfect.

You do not need to have all the answers.

All you need to do is begin.

Take a deep breath. Feel the weight of old stories falling away.

You are ready.

You are the healer your home, your family, and the world has been waiting for.

FINAL CHAPTER

THE PATH AHEAD – YOUR HEALING NEVER ENDS, IT EVOLVES

How Healing Transforms Your Life—A Personal Reflection

Healing is not just about letting go of pain—it is about discovering who you truly are beneath the layers of fear, trauma, and self-doubt.

At the beginning of this journey, healing may have felt like a battle, a struggle to overcome past wounds. But as you have walked through these chapters, you have likely begun to realize that healing is not about fixing yourself—it is about returning to yourself.

This chapter is an invitation to pause, reflect, and acknowledge how far you have come. Because you are not the same person who started this journey.

How Healing Changes You in Ways You Never Expected

As you heal, everything about you shifts—your thoughts, your relationships, your energy.

Here are some of the most profound transformations that happen when you commit to healing:

- **You stop reacting, and start responding.**

Triggers that once caused emotional storms no longer control you. You begin to pause, breathe, and respond from a place of awareness.

- **You attract different people into your life.**

As your energy shifts, so do your relationships. Toxic connections fade, and you start drawing in people who respect, support, and uplift you.

- **You trust yourself more.**

Doubt and fear no longer paralyze you. You begin to listen to your intuition, knowing that you are guided in every step.

- **You feel lighter.**

Healing removes the weight of emotional baggage you have carried for years. Suddenly, life does not feel so heavy—it feels open, expansive, and full of possibility.

- **You no longer seek validation.**

You stop depending on others to make you feel worthy. Instead, you anchor your worth in yourself.

If you take a moment to reflect, you will see that you have already changed in ways you never imagined.

Your Personal Healing Reflection

Let's take a moment to honor your growth. Grab a journal or simply reflect on these questions:

1. What has changed within me since I started this journey?

2. What emotional burdens have I released?

3. What healing lesson impacted me the most?

4. How do I see myself differently now?

As you answer these questions, allow yourself to feel proud. Healing is not easy, but you have done the work.

The Healing Continues—Embracing the Next Chapter

Healing is not a final destination. It is a way of life. You will still have moments of doubt, sadness, or setbacks—but now, you have the tools to navigate them.

The most powerful realization is this:

- You are no longer afraid of your emotions.

- You know how to process and release what no longer serves you.

- You trust that every challenge is leading you to something greater.

This is what healing truly is—the ability to walk through life with openness, trust, and peace.

Final Thought: You Are a Healer, You Are Free

Take a deep breath. You have come so far.

You are no longer trapped in the past. You are no longer defined by old wounds. You are stepping into a life of peace, purpose, and freedom. The journey never ends—but now, you walk it as a healer.

The Continuous Journey of Growth—What Comes Next?

Healing is not a destination, nor is it a finish line you cross with finality. It is a lifelong unfolding, an evolution that draws you deeper into your truth, your light, and your highest potential. If you have reached this part of the book, it is because something within you has awakened. You have traveled through the lessons, the healing, the transformation—and now, you stand at the threshold of something even greater. This is not the end. It is the beginning of something extraordinary.

One day, you will look back and realize that what once felt unbearable has now become your wisdom. The wounds that once consumed you will have transformed into sacred lessons. The emotions that once ruled your life will have become tools of growth, refining you, strengthening you, and preparing you for the next phase of your journey. Growth is not about reaching a point of perfection—it is about stepping into deeper levels of self-awareness, expansion, and alignment. The most profound transformations happen when you realize that healing is not about fixing yourself; it is about remembering who you have always been.

With healing comes clarity, and with clarity comes choice. You will notice shifts in your relationships, in your mindset, in the way you carry yourself. You will no longer chase people, experiences, or validation that no longer serve your highest self. You will begin to trust your intuition more deeply, allowing it to guide you effortlessly toward the life meant for you. Healing is not just about moving on from pain—it is about stepping into a life where you are fully present, fully alive, fully you.

And for some of you, there will be a new calling—a quiet, yet powerful knowing that healing is not just a personal experience but something you are meant to share. A true healer does not force, does not convince, does not push. A true healer becomes the embodiment of light, simply being the change, creating ripples of transformation through their presence alone. You may find yourself drawn to guiding others, holding space for their emotions, offering wisdom, or working with energy in ways you never imagined. Some heal with words, some with touch, some with energy, some simply with their presence. If this calling stirs within you, trust it. It is real. And it is yours to embrace.

For those who feel ready to step into a deeper understanding of healing—not just for themselves, but for others—I invite you to take this journey further with my next book, Amplified Healing. In it, we explore the mastery of healing at a professional level, merging science with spirituality, intuition with structure, and energy with transformation. Healing is not just an act; it is an art. And when you learn to harness it at a deeper level, you do not just change lives—you elevate them.

But even if you do not take the path of a healer, know this: Your healing is never wasted. Every lesson, every breakthrough, every moment of clarity radiates outward, shifting the energy of the world in ways you cannot yet see. You may have healed for yourself, but your healing will touch those around you, perhaps in ways they may never even realize. Healing is not an isolated act—it is a ripple, a movement, a silent revolution that changes the world one soul at a time.

You are no longer the person who started this book. You have shifted, expanded, and awakened. And yet—this is just the beginning. Your journey will never be linear, nor will it ever truly end, for your soul is designed to grow, to evolve, to reach toward something greater with each passing moment. Healing is forever, and so is your growth.

So, as you close this book, I leave you with this: You are ready. You are whole. You are powerful beyond measure. And the best is yet to come.

Happy Healing.
Love and Light,
Madhura Girish

Resources & Tools for Lifelong Healing—Where to Go from Here

Healing is not an endpoint—it is a lifelong commitment to yourself. You have walked through this book, uncovered wounds, and discovered powerful healing techniques. But what happens now? Where do you go from here?

This final chapter is not just about resources—it is about anchoring your transformation, ensuring that you continue growing, evolving, and healing with purpose. Consider this your personalized roadmap for lifelong healing.

1. Honoring How Far You Have Come

Before you think about what is next, take a moment to acknowledge your journey. Healing is not easy. It takes courage to face yourself, to unlearn patterns, and to choose growth over comfort. Yet, you did it. You have come so far.

- Reflect on this: Who were you before you started this book, and who are you now?

- What emotions, beliefs, or fears have you released?

- What new wisdom or healing practices have become a part of your life?

Write it down. Honor your transformation. Because this is not just knowledge—it is your evolution.

2. Creating Your Personal Healing Rituals

Healing is most effective when it becomes a daily, effortless part of your life. Now is the time to create your own personal healing rituals. These are simple, grounding practices that keep you aligned, balanced, and emotionally clear.

- Morning Rituals to Start the Day with Strength & Peace

- Begin with deep breathing or a moment of stillness.

- Set an intention: "Today, I choose peace, healing, and alignment."

- Move your body—stretch, walk, or practice mindful movement.

- Cleanse your energy—light incense, take a cleansing shower, or visualize golden light surrounding you.

- Start the day with gratitude—write down three things you appreciate.

- Evening Rituals to Release & Restore

- Reflect on the day—what did you learn, and what will you release?

- Journal any emotions, thoughts, or insights that surfaced.

- Practice self-compassion—remind yourself, "I am doing my best, and that is enough."

- Engage in an energy-clearing practice (burn sage, take a salt bath, or do deep breathing).

- End the day with a healing affirmation: "I allow my body, mind, and soul to rest, heal, and renew."

Your healing routine should feel natural and effortless—something you return to not out of obligation, but because it nourishes you.

3. Building Your Healing Toolkit

A healer is only as strong as their tools. Your personal healing toolkit should be filled with resources that bring you comfort, clarity, and balance. Consider including:

- **Journaling tools** – A notebook for self-reflection, release, and inner guidance.

- **Meditation & breathwork practices** – Techniques to calm your mind and expand awareness.

- **Crystals & natural elements** – Stones like amethyst for peace, rose quartz for self-love, and black tourmaline for protection.

- **Essential oils & herbal remedies** – Scents like lavender for relaxation, frankincense for spiritual connection, or peppermint for mental clarity.

- **Music & sound healing** – Frequencies, singing bowls, or calming music to shift your energy.

Create a space—whether it's a corner in your room or a small altar—where you can return to for healing whenever needed. Make your environment a sanctuary.

4. Continuing Your Growth & Evolution

Healing is a lifelong journey, and growth is an ongoing process. You are never done learning. Here's how to keep expanding:

- Stay connected to your intuition. Your inner wisdom is always guiding you—listen to it.

- Surround yourself with like-minded souls. Healing is easier when you are supported by those on the same path.

- Be open to new healing modalities. As you evolve, different practices may call to you—trust what resonates.

- Keep practicing self-compassion. Healing is not about being perfect; it is about progress, growth, and self-love.

Final Thought: You Are the Healer You Were Always Seeking

This book was never about teaching you something new—it was about helping you remember who you have always been. A healer. A guide. A powerful, intuitive soul capable of transformation.

Take a deep breath. You have everything you need within you. You do not need to seek outside validation, because you are already whole.

Let this be your final affirmation:

- *"I am my own healer. I am my own guide. I trust my journey, I embrace my growth, and I walk forward with peace, strength, and purpose."*

Go forward, knowing that healing is not something outside of you—it is who you are. And now, it is yours to share.